UNITED NATIONS CONVENTION ON THE RIGHTS OF THE CHILD

FIRST NATIONAL REPORT OF IRELAND

Prepared by the Department of Foreign Affairs
Dublin 2, Ireland.

© Government of Ireland 1996

ISBN 0-7076-2395-2

Table Of Contents

Schedule of Documents supplied with this Report to the UN Committee on the Rights of the Child

United Nations Convention on the Rights of the Child

INTRODUCTION

1. On 30 September 1990, Ireland signed the UN Convention on the Rights of the Child. The Convention was subsequently ratified by Ireland on 21 September 1992, the document of ratification being deposited with the Secretary-General of the United Nations. Ireland showed its commitment to the aims of the Convention by ratifying without any reservation whatsoever. The Convention entered into force for Ireland on 21 October 1992.

2. This 54-article Convention is in essence a "bill of rights" for all children. It is a positive step towards the protection of the human rights of all children in spirit and in letter by having as its guiding principle "the best interests of the child". It aims to create the conditions in which children may take an active and creative part in the social and political life of their countries.

3. Children have a particular vulnerability and are often defenceless against forces that they cannot comprehend. Ireland is committed to achieving the maximum protection possible for the rights of all children. This Convention and its reporting process provide a valuable means of assessing progress.

4. This report has been prepared pursuant to Ireland's obligation under article 44 to present periodic reports to the UN Committee on the Rights of The Child on the protection afforded under Irish law to the rights guaranteed by the Convention. This is Ireland's first national report under the Convention. It was coordinated by the Human Rights Unit in the Political Division of the Department of Foreign Affairs, in cooperation with all Government Departments who deal with child related matters.

5. The basic law of the State is Bunreacht na hÉireann, the Constitution of Ireland, adopted by referendum in 1937. The Constitution states that all legislative, executive and judicial powers of Government derive from the people. It sets out the form of Government and defines the powers of the President and of the Government. The Constitution defines the structure and powers of the Courts and regulates the appointment of the Judiciary. The Constitution also contains a comprehensive code for the protection of human rights and sets out the fundamental rights of the citizen. The definition of rights covers five broad headings: Personal Rights, the Family, Education, Private Property and Religion. The Family occupies a central position in the Constitution and in Irish society, being recognised as the natural, primary and fundamental unit group of society.

6. Ireland is a sovereign, independent, parliamentary democracy. The National Parliament, the Oireachtas, consists of the President and two Houses: a House of Representatives, Dáil Éireann and a Senate, Seanad Éireann. The functions and powers of the President, Dáil and Seanad derive from the Constitution of Ireland. All laws passed by the Oireachtas must conform to the Constitution.

7.   Local government is administered by 113 local authorities funded partly by State grants and partly by local taxes on non-residential property. Local government has responsibility for public housing, water and sanitation, road maintenance, vocational education and certain other services. Under the Health Act, 1970, statutory responsibility for the administration of health services in Ireland is vested in eight regional Health Boards with each Board having responsibility for the administration of health and personal social services in its functional area. Under the Child Care Act 1991, Health Boards have statutory responsibility to promote the welfare of children who are not receiving adequate care and protection.

8.   According to the last full census in 1991, the State had a total population of 3,525,719 inhabitants. In 1994 the population was estimated at 3.571 million. Approximately 44% of the population is under 25 years and 27% is under 15 years. The birth rate in Ireland has been falling steadily since 1980. In 1993, for the first time on record, the total period fertility rate fell below the minimum population replacement rate of 2.1. The rate fell even further in 1994 to 1.9. There were 47,929 births registered in 1994 and if present trends continue, the annual number of births could fall below 40,000 within the next 15 years. This compares with a peak of 74,064 births recorded in 1980.

9.   The minimum voting age in Ireland is 18 years. The electoral system in elections to the Dáil is proportional representation by means of the single transferable vote in multi-seat constituencies. There are 166 members of Dáil Éireann. The single transferable vote is also used for the election of the President, members of the Local Authorities and 49 of the 60 members of the Seanad. The remaining 11 Senators are nominated by the Taoiseach (Prime Minister).

10.   Article 8 of the Constitution provides that the Irish language, as the national language, is the first official language, and that the English language is recognised as a second official language. The Courts have recognised the rights of litigants to conduct their cases through either language. English is the more widely spoken language throughout the country although Irish is spoken as the first language in areas known as the Gaeltacht, situated mainly along the western seaboard. However, Irish speakers are also to be found in all parts of the country. The population (aged three years and over) of the officially defined Gaeltacht in the 1991 census was 79,563, of whom 56,469 or 71% are Irish-speaking. Although Irish speakers are a minority of the population as a whole, the constitutional position of Irish as the first official language and the continued policy of successive governments to revive the Irish language ensures that their rights are protected.

11.   Freedom of thought, conscience, the free profession and practice of religion are guaranteed by the Constitution, subject to public order and morality. The State guarantees not to endow any religion. The majority of Irish people belong to Christian religious denominations. Ninety-three per cent of the population are Roman Catholic and 3.4 per cent belong to various Protestant denominations. There is also a small but long-established Jewish community. In recent years a small Muslim community has

developed, mainly in Dublin. The remainder belong either to smaller religious groups or have no specific religious affiliations.

12. In Ireland there is high life-expectancy, a low death-rate and low infant and maternal mortality. The education system and health services are also of a very high standard. In common with other countries there are problems in the areas of child abuse, homelessness and the care of juvenile offenders.

13. Ireland provides a high quality health service to all Irish residents. Children referred for treatment from child health clinics and school health examinations are exempt from statutory charges; as are children suffering from prescribed diseases and disabilities. Perinatal and infant mortality in Ireland are now at the lowest levels ever achieved and among the lowest in the world. Rates are now less than a third of what they were 30 years ago. For the most recent available year (1991), the perinatal mortality rate stood at 9.9 deaths per 1,000 live and still births.

14. Education is compulsory up to 15 years of age but the Constitution provides for the right of parents to educate their children at home. The White Paper on Education published in April 1994 proposes raising the minimum school-leaving age to 16 years or the completion of three years of junior-cycle education, whichever is later. Over the past 25 years there has been a substantial development of the Irish education system in response to the needs of a rapidly-changing society. There are currently almost one million full-time students in Ireland. There has also been increased involvement of parents in the education of their children. Third-level educational institutions have expanded and developed in Ireland since the mid 1960s. Student numbers have grown from 20,000 in 1965 to almost 90,000 in 1994 and enrolments may be as high as 115,000 by the year 2000.

15. The social welfare system in Ireland is designed to assist individuals and families who are in need. It covers all the internationally recognised forms of social security and incorporates a mix of social insurance and social assistance programmes which provide financial support to people at certain stages of their lives or when specific contingencies arise such as illness, unemployment or widowhood. Total social security expenditure in 1994 was £3,761 million which represented 33.6% of current government expenditure and was equivalent to 12.1% of Gross National Product. Child Benefit is universal and generally paid to the mother or primary carer. Family Income Supplement is paid to assist families on low pay. Families who have a child with a disability are also treated favourably under the social welfare and income tax codes.

16. The principles of the Convention are reflected in Ireland's multilateral and bilateral overseas development assistance policy. Ireland contributes to key multilateral organisations which assist children. A number of overseas programmes specifically relating to the needs of children receive Government funding. Furthermore development projects targeting education and primary health care are being implemented in each of the priority countries for the Irish Aid programme in Africa.

17.   Article 29 of the Constitution sets out Ireland's position in international relations. In particular, sub-section 3 states that

>   "Ireland accepts the generally recognised principles of international law as its rule of conduct in its relations with other states".

18.   Ireland was a founding member of the Council of Europe in 1949, and joined the United Nations in 1955. Ireland is a member state of the European Union and by Article 29.4.3 of the Constitution, has accepted the superiority of European Community law over national law. This includes the submission to the compulsory jurisdiction of an international tribunal, the European Court of Justice.

II. GENERAL MEASURES OF IMPLEMENTATION

A. Measures Taken to Harmonize National Law and Policy with the Provisions of the Convention

19.   Ireland signed the European Convention on the exercise of Children's Rights on 25 January 1996. That Convention is intended to supplement the United Nations Convention on the Rights of the Child. Ireland proposes to ratify the European Convention as quickly as possible.

20.   Both historically and constitutionally the family has been the unit of society which received special protection, and children's rights have been taken into account within this unit. However, the Child Care Act, 1991, marks a movement towards recognising the child as a separate entity with rights distinct from the family. The Act represents a movement away from the concept of children as parental property to an understanding of the child as a person who has rights by virtue of being a child. It is one of the most enlightened pieces of legislation enacted in recent years and updated all earlier legislation to take account of situations of neglect and abuse which have been coming to the fore in Ireland in recent years.

21.   The Act contains 79 sections of which 61 have been brought into operation to date. The main provisions which are in force are contained in Parts I, II, III, IV, V and VI of the Act. The Act is being implemented on a phased basis as the necessary infrastructure was not immediately in place to provide the back up systems needed. However all 79 sections will be in operation by the end of 1996.

22.   The most recent phase in the programme for the implementation of the Act involved the entry into force on the 31 October 1995 of Parts III, IV, V and VI which deal respectively with the protection of children in emergencies, care proceedings and the powers and duties of Health Boards in relation to children in their care. These provisions strengthen the powers of the Health Boards, the Garda Síochána (the police force) and the Courts to intervene in cases of child abuse and neglect. The remaining Parts, which deal with the regulation of children's residential centres and the supervision of pre-school services, will be implemented by the end of 1996. The Government have also made three sets of new regulations relating to the placement by Health Boards of children in foster care, residential care and with relatives. These regulations also came into operation on 31 October 1995.

23.   While it would have been preferable if all provisions of the Child Care Act had entered into force on enactment, the child care services were not in a position to implement all of the Act's provisions immediately. All political parties have recognised the need to put in place a proper infrastructure to support the legislation and to provide the

Health Boards with the extra resources required to enable them to effectively discharge their important new functions under the Act.

24.   For this legislation to be effective it must be backed up by a sustained programme of investment in the development of new child care services and family supports which are capable of responding to the needs of those whom the Act is designed to help. The implementation of Parts III and IV in particular has enormous resource implications. Since 1993 the Government have approved the development and expansion of child care and family support services at a cost of **IR£35 million** on an annual basis. These developments have been targeted at strengthening the capacity of the Health Boards and voluntary agencies to meet the new demands that will arise under the Child Care Act.

25.   The particular vulnerability of children requires special focus on their protection. While the existence of child abuse has never been denied it is only recently that the actual extent of the suffering and pain caused by the problem has come to be fully appreciated. Several high profile cases of appalling abuse have been reported in the Irish media and the scale of the problem has horrified the entire community. Several voluntary non-governmental organisations have played a significant role in alerting and informing the public. As a result awareness of the problem of child abuse has increased enormously.

26.   Steps are being taken to deal with the escalation in complaints of child abuse and neglect. The Government has taken a series of measures designed to protect children and to help the victims of child abuse, one of these being the full implementation of the aforementioned Child Care Act, 1991. This contains a comprehensive statutory framework for the protection of children from abuse and neglect. The key principles of the Act reflect very closely the provisions of the Convention in relation to the right to protection from abuse and the right to proper standards of care. The act aims at ensuring that the best interests of the child are a primary consideration and that the child's right to have due consideration given to his or her wishes is protected.

27.   Health Boards are now under a statutory duty to promote the welfare of children who are not receiving adequate care and protection and the powers of the Health Boards have been strengthened to provide child care and family support services. Where children are in serious danger, improved procedures to facilitate immediate intervention by Health Boards and the Garda Síochána are provided for under the Act. The Act also enables the Courts to place children who have been assaulted, ill-treated, neglected or sexually abused or who are at risk, in the care of or under the supervision of, Health Boards. Provision for the introduction of inspection and supervision of pre-school services and the registration and inspection of residential centres for children are also included in the Act.

28.   A Health Board must, under section 8 of the Act, report annually on the adequacy of the child care and family support services in its area. In preparing this report, the Board must have regard to the needs of children not receiving adequate care and

protection. A copy of this report must be submitted to the Minister for Health. This provides a regular and systematic review of the adequacy of services in its region.

29. Section 11 of the Act gives the Minister for Health, and Health Boards, specific statutory authority to conduct or commission research into child care related matters. A number of Health Boards have already commissioned studies into the various aspects of their current services with a view to developing them in accordance with the requirements of the legislation.

30. Prior to 1991 there had been no domestic Irish legislation governing the issue of foreign adoptions, even though Irish couples adopted children abroad and returned with them to Ireland. The Adoption Act 1991 conforms with the provisions of the Convention regarding intercountry adoptions. The Act sets out new statutory procedures for the adoption of foreign children by Irish residents. It provides important safeguards for the welfare of the child and aims to ensure that full pre-adoption assessment of the prospective adoptive parents is completed before an adoption takes place. This Act also seeks to ensure that an inter-country adoption does not result in any improper financial gain for any of the parties involved.

Health Strategy

31. The Health Strategy published on 21 April 1994 was endorsed by Government in the policy agreement " A Government of Renewal", as the basis for its programme in the health area. The main theme of the Strategy is the re-orientation of the system towards more effectiveness and efficiency by reshaping the way that health services are planned and delivered. The Strategy is underpinned by three important principles, equity, quality of service and accountability and is accompanied by a Four-Year Action Plan which sets out specific targets for each of the main health sectors.

32. All areas identified in the Strategy have been the subject of substantial preparation and achievement since it was launched in 1994. Among the main tasks which have been achieved are the production of a Health Promotion Strategy, a discussion document on Women's Health, and a White Paper on new mental health legislation.

National Anti-Poverty Strategy (NAPS) and Commission on the Family

33. Studies have shown that households with children face a disproportionate risk of poverty in Ireland. One such report was published by the Combat Poverty Agency following research by the Family Studies Centre in University College Dublin. Titled "The Cost of a Child", the study indicated that almost one third of Irish children were substantially dependent on State support for their upbringing and concluded that, without adequate child support payments, covering, at least, the most basic expenditure for the rearing of children, child poverty was likely to remain a significant feature of the Irish economy for an indefinite period of time. The Combat Poverty Agency described the results of the report as disturbing and argued that the

deterioration in the relative position of households with children had implications for child income support policies.

34. To combat such exclusion, the Government announced, in December 1994, its intention to introduce a new type of child income support. This is covered in more detail in Paragraph 416 of this Report. The Minister for Social Welfare has, more recently, appointed a Commission on the Family with a mandate to examine the needs and priorities of the family in a rapidly changing social and economic environment and to make recommendations on how best to facilitate families in the support and development of their individual members. Representatives from the medical, voluntary/NGO, and educational sectors are included in this Commission as are the four Government Departments who mainly deal with social policy - i.e. Social Welfare, Health, Education and Equality and Law Reform. An interim report is expected in October 1996 with the Commission's final report and recommendations due by June 1997.

35. A further significant development was the announcement of a National Anti-Poverty Strategy in April 1995. This decision followed the UN World Summit for Social Development in Copenhagen at which the Irish Government endorsed a programme of action geared both to eliminating absolute poverty in the developing world and the substantial reduction of overall poverty and inequalities everywhere.

36. A key objective of the Strategy is that it will become automatic practice that all policies and programmes are assessed for their impact on poverty and that the reduction and prevention of poverty and social exclusion be clearly identified as key objectives for all Government departments and agencies.

37. The Strategy is being developed by an Inter-Departmental Policy Committee chaired by the Department of the Taoiseach, with the Department of Social Welfare providing the Deputy Chair. The Secretariat is being augmented by the Combat Poverty Agency which plays a key advisory role in the process. The Committee has been charged with preparing a report which will form part of the National Report to the United Nations, to be completed before the end of 1996, to demonstrate national progress in implementing the UN Commitments arising from the World Summit.

38. The Committee invited submissions from interested parties. The first stage of the Committee's work has now been completed with the production of three documents:-

A. **Summary of submissions made by voluntary and community organisations on the NAPs**

The report analyses 241 submissions made by (mainly) voluntary and community organisations in relation to the NAPs. **Education** emerged as the area most often emphasised in the submission as having a key role in combatting poverty and social exclusion. Other policy areas raised in a significant number of submissions are:

- Social Welfare, Taxation and income support;

- Employment & enterprise, including long-term unemployment;

- Training;

- Health;

- Housing and Homelessness;

- Community Development, urban and rural poverty.

B.   **Consultation Paper on Institutional Mechanisms to Support the National Anti-Poverty Strategy**

This paper looks at possible institutional mechanisms for implementing and monitoring the National Anti-Poverty Strategy. It does not make recommendations, but raises issues and invites feedback on how to put in place the most effective mechanisms for successful implementation of the Strategy.

C.   **Summary of an Overview Statement on the National Anti-Poverty Strategy**

The Summary has been prepared to encourage further debate and consideration prior to finalisation of the Overview Statement by the Committee.

39.   These three papers are now being discussed with a wide number of groups with a view to facilitating debate on the issues raised and moving to the next stage of the process, i.e. the development of key themes and priority areas which the strategy should address. Participation of people with personal experience of poverty, through the organisations that represent them, will continue to be a key feature of the development of the National Anti-Poverty Strategy as it moves on to the next stage.

Unemployment

40.   It is clear that unemployment is a significant factor in child poverty and can have deleterious consequences for a child's enjoyment of the rights promoted and protected by this Convention. There are several Government initiatives aimed at reducing unemployment (particularly long term unemployment) in the community. The 1996 Budget introduced a package of pro-employment measures including:

- enhancements to the existing concessions available to employers, employees and the self-employed in relation to their Pay Related Social Insurance contributions;

- further improvements in the qualifying conditions for the Family Income Supplement scheme;

- retention of the Child Dependent Allowance for a 13 week period for unemployed people who have been unemployed for 12 months and who take up work which is expected to last for at least 4 weeks;

- simplification of and improvement in the method of assessment of entitlement for Unemployment Assistance; and

- an extension to the Back to Work Allowance Scheme;

Education Policy

41. Article 42 of the Constitution acknowledges that the primary and natural educator of the child is the family and guarantees to respect the inalienable right and duty of parents to provide, according to their means, for the religious and moral, intellectual, physical and social education of their children. Parents are free to provide this education in their homes or in private schools, or in schools recognised or established by the State.

42. The Constitution contains the basic provisions on the right to education and these provisions are implemented by circular and directive, providing the framework within which schools operate.

43. The Government's White Paper, **Charting our Education Future**, published in April 1995, proposes a comprehensive, radical reform of the Irish education system. A number of important principles underpin the approach to the White Paper. These include the promotion of quality, equality, pluralism, partnership and accountability. These principles are promoted within a framework which requires the State to protect and promote fundamental human and civil rights, to promote the holistic development of individual students and to empower their fullest participation in society and the economy.

44. The White Paper envisages new institutional and organisational arrangements for the delivery of education services. At school level, Boards of Management will be established for all first and second level schools in receipt of government funding. Major changes in relation to in-school management will be implemented. The White Paper also proposes the establishment of new regional education structures - Education Boards - which will be established subject to the agreement of the Government. These Boards will be responsible for the planning and coordination of educational provisions

in their regions. The Boards will be representative of school patrons, trustees, owners, governors, parents, teachers, public representatives, Ministerial nominees and the wider community.

45. It is intended that the proposals set out in the White Paper will be underpinned by legislation and will provide a comprehensive framework for educational development at the end of the twentieth century.

B. Existing or Planned Mechanisms at National or Local Level for Co-ordinating Policies Relating to Children and for Monitoring the Implementation of the Convention

46. In accordance with the responsibility of the Government for implementing the provisions of the Convention, each Department of State implements those provisions of the Convention which fall into its particular area of responsibility. The production of this report involved all Departments reflecting on how policies in areas of relevance to them are consistent with the provisions of the Convention.

47. Child care services by their nature cover a broad spectrum of issues which concern not only a number of Government Departments but also many statutory bodies and voluntary agencies. At a national level, there have been difficulties in achieving a coordinated approach across the various strands of the services and in the integration of policies that transcend government departmental boundaries.

Coordination of Child Care Services

48. In recognition of this difficulty and in accordance with a commitment given in the Programme for Government, A Government of Renewal, December 1994, the Irish Government has appointed a **Minister of State to the Departments of Health, Education and Justice** with special responsibility for children and in particular co-ordinating the activities of the three Departments in relation to child protection and juvenile justice. The Minister of State has also been charged with responsibility for addressing the problems of school truancy and early school leavers as well as having responsibility for overseeing the full implementation of the Child Care Act. This appointment has, for the first time, brought together under a single Minister responsibility for child protection, youth homelessness, school truancy and children in trouble with the law, areas which in the past have been the responsibility of three government Ministers.

49. The Minister is involved in the preparation of new legislation in the area of juvenile justice, the purpose of which is to streamline the process of early intervention and to provide for the Courts a range of community based sanctions and measures for child offenders. In addition it will deal with the need for suitable custodial facilities for child offenders where detention of a child has to be imposed as a last resort. Parents will also be involved in dealing with situations where their children come into conflict with the law.

50.	At an operational level, an inter-departmental committee representative of the three Departments, Health, Education and Justice and chaired by the Minister of State has been established. The initiative is paying dividends in terms of closer working relationships between the three Departments and their agencies and is resulting in a more cohesive approach to problem solving and policy development.

51.	Ireland is the first country in Europe to appoint a Minister with special responsibility for Children. The measure reflects the special priority accorded by the Government to the development of child care services in order to more adequately address the needs of our children.

52.	Each Health Board is required, under section 7 of the Child Care Act, to establish a Child Care Advisory Committee to advise the Health Board on the provision of child and family support services in its area. The role of Child Care Advisory Committees is to monitor the provision of child care services at local level and the fulfilment by the Health Boards of their obligations under the Child Care Act. Each committee must report to the Health Board on the services in the area and consult with the voluntary non-governmental bodies providing services in the region. It also has a function in reviewing the needs of children who are not receiving adequate care and protection.

53.	Membership of the Child Care Advisory Committees includes persons with a special interest or expertise in child welfare; there is one representative each of the Gardaí, the Probation and Welfare Service and the educational sector. In order to ensure that voluntary bodies are given an effective voice and role in the planning and development of services, the legislation provides that each committee must include representatives of voluntary non-governmental bodies providing child care and family support services in the region. It is anticipated that consultation of this nature at a regional level will lead to the full development of the necessary services and will ensure that the needs of children are being adequately addressed.

Child Care Policy Unit

54.	In 1993 a Child Care Policy Unit was established in the Department of Health. The Unit holds primary responsibility for the formulation of policy in the area of child care and family welfare with particular reference to child abuse, youth homelessness and family violence. It also oversees the delivery of appropriate services through the Health Boards and voluntary agencies.

55.	Since 1993 the Child Care Policy Unit, in consultation with the eight regional Health Boards, has launched a major programme of developments in child care services. These new initiatives include the creation of over 850 new posts for child care services. The Department of Health has approved, in consultation with the Health Boards, a range of important new developments which are designed to ensure:-

- Ireland's child protection services are strengthened and equipped to respond to the needs of children who are not receiving adequate care and protection,

- Intensive counselling and treatment is provided for victims of child abuse,

- Special therapeutic care is provided for those who have been damaged by abuse and neglect,

- An adequate range of accommodation and supports is available to help homeless young people,

- Children in foster care and residential care are supervised and monitored on a systematic basis, and

- Locally-based helping services are in place to assist families in difficulty.

56. A research project will be undertaken to explore options concerning an appropriate mechanism to promote and protect children's rights in Ireland. The project will be managed by a non-governmental organisation, the Children's Rights Alliance. The terms of reference of the research project will be to examine how arrangements for promoting and protecting children's rights in other countries could have relevance for the situation in Ireland and to make recommendations concerning appropriate options for this country. The Department of Health has confirmed that a grant of £10,000 will be provided to part-fund the research project. The proposed research project represents an important first step in establishing an appropriate mechanism to ensure that children's rights are protected and promoted and should provide some reassurance to many people who are concerned about children's welfare throughout the country.

C.   International Co-operation

57. The principles of the Convention are reflected in Ireland's bilateral and multilateral programmes. In the context of the expansion of Ireland's Overseas Development Aid Programme, voluntary contributions to the UN development agencies were increased by 80% in 1994.

58. Ireland contributes to key multilateral organisations which assist children. These organisations include the United Nations Children's Fund (UNICEF), the World Health Organisation (WHO), the WHO's Children Vaccine Initiative, the United Nations Population Fund (UNPFA), the United Nations High Commissioner for Refugees (UNHCR), the International Organisation for Migration (IOM) to which Ireland was admitted as an observer member in 1992, the World Food Programme (WFP) and the World Bank.

59. A number of overseas programmes specifically relating to the needs of children have received Government funding. In 1994 the Irish Government gave substantial financial

support to emergency humanitarian assistance and rehabilitation type projects, which targeted women and children. In recognition of the appalling consequences which land mines have on children and families in developing countries, Ireland contributed to de-mining clearance projects in Cambodia, Angola and Mozambique.

60.   Furthermore development projects targeting education and primary health care are being implemented in each of the priority countries for the Irish Aid programme in Africa. Under the Primary Health Care component of many Irish Aid projects, particular attention is devoted to mother and child health through training programmes for traditional birth attendants and mother and child health workers, and through support for MCH (mother and child) clinics and dispensaries and nutrition education. Considerable emphasis is also placed on perinatal health. Ireland has granted aid to the construction of a series of satellite maternity clinics and to the provision of training to upgrade midwives' skills and status.

Beijing Conference

61.   Ireland actively participated in negotiations leading to the adoption of the Declaration and Platform for Action by the Fourth World Conference on Women, in Beijing in September 1995. Ireland fully endorses and supports the texts adopted. Chapter IV (L) of the Platform for Action outlines the extent of the problem of ongoing discrimination against the Girl Child, and actions required to combat this discrimination. Irish Aid is currently in the process of finalising Gender Guidelines design implementation and evaluation of its programmes and projects. These guidelines will, inter alia, take into account the results of the Beijing Conference.

D.   Publicizing the Provisions of the Convention under Article 42

62.   All Government Departments and agencies have been made fully aware of the detailed provisions of the Convention. Copies have also been distributed to all primary and secondary schools (approximately 4,200) in Ireland as well as to all public libraries.

E.   Publicizing this Report under Article 44.6

63.   Ireland's report will be published and made available to the general public. Copies will also be circulated to all Government Departments, members of Dáil Éireann, Seanad Éireann, Government Offices and public libraries.

III.   DEFINITION OF THE CHILD

Majority.

64.   In Ireland, the Age of Majority Act, 1985 provides that majority is attained at the age of eighteen years or on marriage. At this age citizens also have the right to vote.

Child Care Act

65.   The Child Care Act, 1991 defines a child as meaning "a person under the age of 18 years other than a person who is or has been married".

Adoption

66.   Under the Adoption Acts a child being considered for adoption must be under 18 years.

Mental Treatment Act

67.   Under the Mental Treatment Act, 1945, as amended, a child is defined as a person under the age of 16 years. The Government has proposed in a White Paper on a new Mental Health Act to define a child for the purpose of mental health legislation as a person who has not yet attained his or her 18th year unless he or she has been married. This would bring the definition in line with child care legislation and with the age of majority.

Legal counselling without parental consent.

68.   A child may sue in court through a "next friend" in some civil law proceedings. However, there are no statutory provisions which empower a child as a plaintiff, to institute family law proceedings (even through a next friend).

Compulsory education.

69.   The School Attendance Act, 1926 and its amendments require children to attend school between the ages of 6 and 15 years. A review of the School Attendance Act which will, in particular, raise the minimum school-leaving age to 16 years in line with the provisions of the White Paper on Education, is currently under-way.

Employment.

70.   The employment of children under the school leaving age is generally prohibited. An exception is made where he/she is a full time student at an institute of secondary education and is participating in a work experience course or other similar educational course arranged or approved by the Minister for Education. However, a child of 14

years but under the school leaving age of 15 years, may be permitted to do light, non-industrial, work during the school holidays. Where a 14 year old child is employed in these limited circumstances it is only permitted on work which is not harmful to health or normal development and does not interfere with the child's schooling. Before employing a child aged 14 to 15 years, the employer must obtain written permission from the child's parent or guardian. The Protection of Young Persons (Employment) Bill, 1996, proposes to raise the legal full-time working age from fifteen to sixteen.

Hazardous Employment.

71.   The Safety, Health and Welfare at Work Act, 1989 imposes a general duty of care on employers in relation to all employees. The provisions of the 1989 Act are amplified by the Safety, Health and Welfare at Work (General Application) Regulations 1993. These Regulations also impose a particular duty on employers to ensure that sensitive risk groups of employees, which would include children, are protected against any dangers which would specifically affect them.

Sexual consent.

72.   Outside of marriage, 17 years is the age of consent for both heterosexual and homosexual intercourse.

Marriage.

73.   The current minimum age for marriage is 16 years. The High Court may grant exemption from this requirement. Under section 1 of the Marriages Act, 1972 a marriage involving a party under 16 years which had not received the requisite court approval would be void. Those under 21 years who wish to marry are, with certain exceptions, legally obliged to obtain the consent of parents or, where appropriate, guardians. The Family Law Act 1994, increases the minimum age of marriage to 18 years and removes any requirement for parental consent. It also provides for a minimum period of notice of marriage of 3 months. There is provision for exemption by court order of the notice requirement to meet situations where the inflexible application of the requirement would be unfair.

Voluntary enlistment in the armed forces.

74.   In Ireland, there is no conscription into the Defence Forces. The general rule with regard to enlistment is that a person under the age of 18 years (other than a person who is or has been married) may not be enlisted until the consent of his/her parent, guardian or other person in loco parentis, has been obtained (see also paragraph 536).

Voluntarily giving evidence in court.

75.   In any criminal proceedings, the evidence of a person under 14 years of age may be received otherwise than on oath or affirmation if the court is satisfied that the child is

capable of giving an intelligible account of events which are relevant to those proceedings. In civil proceedings, witnesses are not subject to any age limit, but evidence must be given on oath or by affirmation.

Criminal liability.

76.   There is a conclusive presumption in Irish law that a child under 7 years is incapable of committing an offence. There is a rebuttable presumption that a child between 7 and 14 years is incapable of committing an offence, i.e. it must be proved not only that the child committed the offence but that he or she knew that it was wrong. These ages are being reviewed in the context of the examination of the juvenile justice system currently taking place.

Deprivation of liberty/imprisonment.

77.   Males under 16 and females under 17 cannot, except in exceptional circumstances be sent to prisons or places of detention operated by the Department of Justice. Under those ages, young offenders may be detained in special schools operated by the Department of Education (see paragraphs 555 to 570 for details).

Consumption of alcohol and controlled substances.

78.   The Intoxicating Liquor Act, 1988 provides protection for children against alcohol abuse. It does this by making it an offence:

- for any person under 18 years of age to purchase alcohol, or to consume it in any place other than a private residence;

- for any person to purchase alcohol for consumption by a person under 18 years of age in any place other than a private residence;

- for a licence holder to sell or deliver alcohol to a person under 18 years of age or to permit consumption of alcohol by, or the supply of alcohol to, persons under 18; and

In addition

- alcohol in the possession of persons under 18 years of age in any place other than a private residence may be seized by the Gardaí;

- persons under 15 years of age are not allowed into the licensed portion of a licensed premises unless accompanied by a parent or guardian;

- persons under 18 years of age are not allowed in the part of a licensed premises where an extension permitting late night drinking is in force;

- persons under 18 years of age are not allowed into off-licensed premises (where alcohol is sold for consumption off the premises) unless accompanied by a parent or guardian.

Abuse of Solvents.

79. Section 74 of the Child Care Act, 1991, which was implemented in 1991, makes it an offence to sell solvent based products to children where it is known or suspected that they will be abused. It also gives the Gardaí power to seize any substance in the possession of a child in a public place which the Gardaí have reasonable cause to believe is being misused by that child in a manner likely to cause him to be intoxicated.

Underage Smoking.

80. The 1988 Tobacco (Health Promotion and Protection) Act makes it an offence to sell any tobacco product to a person under 16 years of age.

Social Welfare Provisions.

81. Within the Social Welfare code, the concept of dependency is normally defined as the economic dependence of a person arising from the various social security contingencies, e.g. unemployment, retirement, illness, old age, etc. In relation to such persons, dependency also covers their dependent spouse and children who are wholly or mainly maintained by them.

82. Accordingly, under Social Welfare legislation, financial support is provided, under this concept of dependency, for children under the age of 16. Entitlement may continue, depending on the nature of the benefit/allowance, to ages 18 or 22, where the child is in full time education or undertaking courses run by FÁS, the State's employment training authority, or has a physical disability or a mental handicap.

83. Children under 16 years of age, if employed, are not liable for Pay Related Social Insurance but cover is nevertheless provided for certain Occupational Injuries Benefits.

Child Benefit

84. Child Benefit is normally paid up to 16 years of age in respect of a child but is extended for 18 year olds who are in full-time education or on FÁS (Youthreach) courses.

Maintenance

85. Maintenance is payable in respect of a child until the child reaches 16 years or if the child is in full time education, 21 years.

IV. GENERAL PRINCIPLES

A.   Non-Discrimination (Art. 2)

86.   The Constitution of Ireland provides a general guarantee of equality before the law. Article 40.1 reads as follows:

> "All citizens shall, as human persons, be held equal before the law. This shall not be held to mean that the State shall not in its enactments have due regard to difference of capacity, physical and moral, and of social function."

87.   This guarantee of equality, based on human personality, is as applicable to children as to adults. Discrimination based on a parent's status would be inconsistent with the guarantee of equality in the Constitution as would discrimination based directly on the child's own status.

88.   The Constitution protects the dignity of citizens against discrimination by the State based on race, colour, religion, political or other opinion, national or social origin, property, birth or other status.

89.   There has been a considerable number of cases in which the provisions of Article 40.1 have been invoked before the Courts. In none of these, however, has the alleged inequality before the law been based on race, colour, political or other opinion, national or social origin, or property. However this cannot be taken as an indication that such discrimination does not take place. The legislation currently in force, and proposed legislation in this area, have as their aim the provision of a suitable legal framework which will discourage such discrimination and provide appropriate remedies, where necessary.

90.   The Employment Equality Act, 1977, makes it unlawful to discriminate on grounds of sex or marital status in relation to recruitment for employment, conditions of employment, training or in the matter of opportunities for promotion.

91.   Legislation is currently being drafted prohibiting discrimination on grounds of gender, marital status, family status, sexual orientation, religion, age, disability, race, colour, nationality, national or ethnic origin and membership of the Travelling Community (i.e. a community which has traditionally followed a nomadic lifestyle). The legislation, consisting of two Bills, will cover employment and non-employment areas such as the provision of goods, facilities and services, including recreational facilities and services, entertainment, the provision of education, disposal of property and provision of accommodation, transport and professional services.

92.   The Status of Children Act, 1987 removed discrimination in the law as between children born within and outside marriage. It puts children born outside marriage on the same footing as those born within marriage in the areas of guardianship, maintenance and inheritance. It introduces a statutory procedure to enable any person

to obtain a court declaration as to his parentage and provides for the use of blood tests in determining parentage in civil proceedings.

93.   An unmarried father now has the right to apply to the Court to be appointed a guardian and a special informal procedure has been set up for such applications where the mother consents and the father is registered as such on the births register.

94.   The procedures for having the father's name entered on the births register where he is not married to the mother have also been eased.

B.   Best Interests of the Child (Art. 3)

95.   The requirement that the "best interests of the child" be the guiding principle in all matters affecting "child welfare" underlies the provision of child care services in Ireland. It is clearly enshrined in section 3 of the Child Care Act, 1991 which places a statutory duty on Health Boards to promote the welfare of children who are not receiving adequate care and protection. In the performance of this function, section 3 requires that a Health Board shall have regard to the welfare of the child as the first and paramount consideration. Section 24 imposes a similar obligation on the Courts when hearing proceedings in relation to the care and protection of a child.

Custody Disputes

96.   All Court proceedings which involve the custody of a child are governed by the Guardianship of Infants Act 1964. The "best interests" principle is the paramount consideration in deciding matters of this nature. This is specifically provided for in section 3 of the Guardianship of Infants Act, 1964

97.   Each case involving a custody dispute is unique and account is taken of the entire picture presented to the court. In the case of young children, it has generally been the case that custody of a child will be awarded to the mother. This appears to derive from two considerations. Firstly, there is the assumption that for biological reasons a mother is better able to respond to physical and emotional needs, particularly in the case of a very young child. Secondly, in many cases only the mother has been in a position to care for the infant on a full-time basis. However, there have been some cases in which young children have been placed in the custody of a father and in this regard there is also an increasing awareness that fathers have the capacity to parent young children.

98.   The principle of maintaining family unity is also taken into account by the courts. There have been many cases in which judges have expressed a preference not to separate children, based on the belief that the companionship of brothers and sisters is almost always beneficial for a child. The need to provide stability in the life of a child is also often emphasised. For this reason the Court will usually be reluctant to disturb a custody arrangement which has been in place for a substantial length of time.

Other factors such as educational arrangements, the conduct of parents towards each other, parental conduct towards a child and the religious upbringing of a child are also taken into account.

99.   Section 11 (5) of the Guardianship of Infants Act 1964 (as inserted by section 40 of the Judicial Separation and Family Law Reform Act, 1989) allows the Court of its own motion or on application to it, to procure a report on any question affecting the welfare of a child in guardianship proceedings. The Court may request a suitable person (usually the Probation and Welfare Service or a Health Board) to prepare such a report. The Family Law Act, 1994 gives the Courts power to order a report from either the Probation and Welfare Service or a Health Board and extends those powers of the Court to all family law proceedings. The Bill in effect puts the reporting role of social workers and welfare officers in family law proceedings on a statutory basis.

Foster Care

100.   The Child Care (Placement of Children in Foster Care) Regulations 1995 set out requirements to be complied with by Health Boards in relation to the placing of children in foster care, the supervision, review and visiting of foster children and the removal of children from placements in accordance with the relevant provisions of the Child Care Act. The regulations entered into force on 31 October 1995 and require a Health Board to regard the welfare of the child as the first and paramount consideration when making arrangements for the placement of a child in foster care.

Residential Care

101.   The Child Care (Placement of Children in Residential Care) Regulations 1995 deal with the placing of children in residential care, the supervision, review and visiting of such children and the removal of children from residential placements in accordance with the relevant provisions of the Child Care Act. The Health Boards are required, among other matters, to satisfy themselves that appropriate standards, care practices and operational policies apply in residential centres catering for children placed by the Boards. There is also be a duty on Health Boards to supervise and monitor the children in residential care on a systematic basis.

Adoption

102.   Legislation in force on adoption also embodies the principle that the welfare of the child must be paramount in all decisions made in relation to the placement of a child for adoption and in effecting any subsequent adoption.

Mental Health

103.   Under current mental health legislation a person under 16 years cannot be admitted for psychiatric care without the consent of his or her parent(s) or guardian(s) unless the child is a "Ward of Court". Each in-patient psychiatric centre must be designated as

registered for that purpose by a Health Board or by the Minister for Health. A system of inspection is in operation primarily to protect patients in psychiatric hospitals. This system of inspection also applies to child patients. In general mental health services for children are provided on an out-patient basis in child and family guidance services.

C.   Right to Life (Art.6)

104.   Articles 40.3.2 and 3 of the Constitution provide as follows:

> 2°   The State shall, in particular, by its laws protect as best it may from unjust attack and, in the case of injustice done, vindicate the life ... of every citizen.

> 3°   The State acknowledges the right to life of the unborn and, with due regard to the equal right to life of the mother, guarantees in its laws to respect and, as far as practicable, by its laws to defend and vindicate that right."

105.   Attacks on or threats to life, are covered by a wide range of provisions. Among offences for which severe penalties are provided for are genocide, murder, manslaughter, kidnapping, dangerous driving and serious assaults.

106.   Perinatal and infant mortality is dealt with at Paragraph 294.

Right to Life of Unborn

107.   The right to life of the unborn was inserted into the Constitution following the enactment of the Eighth Amendment to the Constitution Act, 1983. This amendment was effected in the manner prescribed by Article 46 of the Constitution, namely, by means of a Bill passed by both Houses of the Oireachtas and approved by a majority of those citizens who voted in a referendum.

108.   Following a High Court hearing the Supreme Court held on appeal in the case of Attorney-General -v- X and others [1992] IR 1 & [1992] IR 16 that termination of pregnancy is permissible in the State where there is a real and substantial risk to the life, as distinct from the health, of the mother which can only be avoided by such termination and that a risk of suicide may constitute a real and substantial risk. The Court also decided in the same case that, while an injunction would not be given to restrain a woman from travelling abroad to obtain an abortion where there is a real and substantial risk to her life, such an injunction could be given to restrain travel abroad to obtain an abortion where there was no such risk. In earlier cases the Court also decided that the dissemination of information on abortion was unlawful having regard to Article 40.3.3 of the Constitution.

109.   In 1992, the thirteenth and fourteenth Amendments to the Constitution were inserted by referendum into Article 40.3.3. They read as follows:

>   "This subsection shall not limit freedom to travel between the State and another state.

>   "This subsection shall not limit freedom to obtain or make available, in the State, subject to such conditions as may be laid down by law, information relating to services lawfully available in another state."

110.   Following the insertion of these Amendments to the Constitution, the Oireachtas enacted The Regulation of Information (Services outside the State for Termination of Pregnancies) Bill, 1995. Before the Bill was signed into law it was referred to the Supreme Court for a decision on whether it or any of its provisions, were unconstitutional.

111.   The Supreme Court reaffirmed its decision in the X Case: that where there is a real and substantial risk to the life, as distinct from the health, of the mother an abortion may be carried out. This position was found to be unaltered by either the thirteenth Amendment (dealing with travel) or the fourteenth Amendment (relating to information) of the Constitution or by the Bill before the Court. The Court also outlined the position of pregnant women (not in the category of X) with regard to abortion information. It found that while a doctor must not advocate or promote the termination of her pregnancy, he/she may give information on abortion services lawfully available outside the State provided that it is given in the context of full information, advice and counselling on all courses of action open to her, including abortion. The final decision, on the course of action to be taken, is left to the woman. A doctor cannot make an appointment with an abortion service on behalf of a woman but once it is made he/she may communicate in the normal way with another doctor with regard to the condition of his/her patient, provided that such communication does not in any way advocate or promote the termination of pregnancy.

Teenage Suicide

112.   The Criminal Law (Suicide) Act 1993 abolished the offence of suicide but it continues to be an offence to be an accomplice to suicide.

113.   There has been a rise in the number of reported deaths from suicide in Ireland between 1970 and 1994. This increase has not been accompanied by a fall in the recorded number of accidental deaths from causes such as poisoning or drowning. Nor has there been a fall in the number of open verdicts in Coroners Courts. It is accepted that there has been a genuine rise in suicide. This rise in the number of reported deaths from suicide has also occurred in the child adolescent age group, although from a very low base.

114. The health strategy document, <u>Shaping a Healthier Future</u>, expressed concern about the increase in the rate of suicide, especially among young people, in Ireland. The World Health Organisation in its <u>Targets for Health for All</u> has recommended action to reverse the rising trend in suicide by the year 2000. It highlights the importance of early detection and treatment for depression, alcoholism and schizophrenia. These concerns are being addressed in the context of the re-organisation of the mental health services in the health strategy.

115. The World Health Organisation also suggest the need for improvements in the underlying societal factors that put a strain on the individual, such as family stress, social isolation and failure at school. It emphasises the need to develop the individual's ability to cope with life events. This ability is a crucial factor in preventing and managing mental illness. The Health Promotion Unit of the Department of Health and the Department of Education are already involved in the delivery of health education programmes for young people, both in school and out of school settings.

116. A national study is being undertaken to establish the incidence and associated factors of suicide to improve the present knowledge base and to facilitate planning of prevention strategies. The Department of Health is contributing towards the cost of a pilot project whose aim is to reduce the occurrence of para-suicide (attempted suicide) and to develop intervention skills which may be applied in this area. The study is being undertaken in collaboration with the WHO-EURO Multi Centre on Para-suicide.

D.   <u>Respect for the Views of the Child (Art.12)</u>

117. One of the primary principles of the Child Care Act, 1991 is to ensure that the wishes of the child are respected where legal proceedings are taken under the terms of this Act.

118. Section 24 of the Child Care Act places a duty on the Courts to take into consideration the wishes of the child in any court proceedings under the Act concerning the child's care or welfare, having regard to the age and understanding of the child.

119. Under section 30(2) of the Child Care Act, a Court will be in a position to facilitate a child's request if the child wishes to attend at a court hearing in proceedings in his or her case. However, this section also makes provision for the Court to refuse such a request if it considers that having regard to the age of the child and the nature of the proceedings it would not be in the best interests of the child.

120. Section 17(2) of the Guardianship of Infants Act, 1964 provides that the wishes of the child may be taken into account by the Court and in order to ascertain these wishes the Court may interview the child. In the case of an older child in particular, his or her wishes may have a decisive influence on the question of custody and access. Such interviews generally take place in an informal setting such as the Judge's chambers. Not only what is said by the child at such interviews but also his or her general

behaviour or demeanour may influence the Court and form part of the basis of any decision of the Court.

Residential Care

(see also paragraph 101 on this issue)

121. The Child Care (Placement of Children in Residential Care) Regulations 1995 require Health Boards to give due consideration to the wishes of a child, having regard to his/her age and understanding, in any matter relating to the placement of a child in residential care, the review of such a placement or the removal of a child from residential care. The Department of Health issued Draft Guidelines on Standards for Children's Residential Centres in January 1995. These Guidelines have been issued to all interest groups in the area for their comment before finalisation. They focus on the child as an individual and emphasise the need for due consideration to be given to the wishes of the child in any arrangements for his or her care. The unique worth and individuality of each child is recognised in the Guidelines and they acknowledge the important contribution to be made by the child in relation to his/her care. They also recommend that children's views and opinions are actively sought and are used to help inform care practices and care planning.

122. The child's right to be heard is clearly identified in the Draft Guidelines on Standards and it is recommended that procedures are put in place in each residential centre to ensure that children in care are facilitated in the expression of any complaints they might have regarding their care.

Adoption

123. The Adoption Acts make provision for the wishes of the child to be taken into consideration where a child is more than 7 years of age at the date of the application for the adoption order.

Mental Health

124. The treatment of mental health problems in children and adolescents takes place mainly on an out-patient basis but a small number may require admission to a residential setting for assessment and/or treatment. A White Paper on Mental Health Legislation was published in August, 1995. It proposes to provide for the admission, by way of court order, of a child who objects to involuntary admission to a designated psychiatric centre but whose parents agree to the admission. Where parents do not consent to treatment, court proceedings will be held to determine whether or not a court order should be made admitting the child to hospital. In such proceedings the child will have an opportunity to express his or her own views. The child will also be provided with separate legal representation.

Judicial Proceedings

125. Under the Criminal Evidence Act, 1992, in cases involving sexual offences or violence, witnesses under 17 years of age may give evidence and be cross-examined through a live television link. In addition, such witnesses may give evidence through a live television link at a preliminary hearing of a case before a District Court.

126. For the purposes of giving evidence through this system, which is known as Video-Link, the witness is located in a special witness room set up for that purpose outside of the courtroom. It means that the witness does not have to go into the courtroom with its often intimidating atmosphere or see the defendant. The system, as far as is technically possible, allows the court proceedings to be conducted as if the witness were giving evidence in the courtroom while at the same time protecting the witness.

127. The special witness room has a waiting room attached which has been carefully furnished with the needs of children in mind. The witness is attended by a special court usher prior to and during the trial. The usher acquaints the witness and others such as his or her parents with the operation of the witness room facilities and the Video-Link.

128. The system which is currently in operation in the Dublin Metropolitan District Court, the Dublin Circuit Court and the Central Criminal Court was introduced on a pilot basis in late 1993. No decision has yet been taken to extend it to provincial venues. However, proceedings being heard in a court which does not have Video-Link facilities can be transferred to a court which has the necessary facilities.

129. Where a person under 17 years gives evidence by Video-Link at a preliminary examination, a video-recording of that evidence is admissible at the trial. In addition, a video-recording of a statement given by a child under 14 years to the Gardaí or other competent persons can in certain circumstances be admitted at trial.

Employment Appeals Tribunal

130. An Employment Appeals Tribunal operates in Ireland in the area of employment protection legislation. In order to be eligible to take a dispute before the Tribunal, a child would have to be or have been in employment which fulfilled the requirements of the various pieces of legislation. This requirement is common to all prospective applicants and any such child would be covered in the same way as anyone else regarding the opportunity to be heard and/or represented before the Tribunal.

V. CIVIL RIGHTS AND FREEDOMS

A. Name and Nationality (Art.7)

131. A child born in Ireland (either in the State or of an Irish citizen in Northern Ireland) or on an Irish ship or aircraft automatically acquires Irish citizenship (the jus soli rule).

132. A person of non-Irish parentage who is born in Northern Ireland since 1922 acquires Irish citizenship merely by making or by having made for them the prescribed declaration. Another mode is by the "jus sanguinis" method. Anyone who at birth has a mother or father possessing Irish citizenship is an Irish citizen, subject to certain qualifications.

133. Adoption by an Irish citizen in accordance with the procedures laid down in the Adoption Acts, 1952-91, also confers Irish nationality. A foreign adoption, effected in favour of an Irish citizen, which is recognised in accordance with the provisions of the Adoption Act, 1991 also confers Irish nationality on the adopted child.

134. Citizenship can also be acquired by naturalisation. This applies to adult aliens or to children whose parents are Irish by descent or naturalised Irish citizens. To facilitate the naturalisation of children, a shorter, less detailed application form is used. Furthermore, the fee to be paid is reduced in the case of children from IR£500 to IR£100. In order to provide that a family can have a common citizenship, and as a matter of administrative practice, applications from children are generally given priority.

135. The obligations imposed under Article 7 of the Convention in relation to the registration of births are complied with by Ireland through the legislative arrangements providing for the civil registration of births. Section 30 of the Registration of Births and Deaths (Ireland) Act, 1863, and section 1 of the Births and Deaths Registration Act (Ireland) 1880, imposes obligations on Registrars and Qualified Informants respectively.

136. This legislation, together with the fact that the vast majority of births take place in maternity hospitals/units has the effect of ensuring that the almost all births are registered immediately after their occurrence. Furthermore the provision of child benefit under the Social Welfare Code on a universal basis has the effect of motivating parents to ensure that births are registered promptly.

B. Preservation of Identity (Art. 8)

137. A child may only be deprived of Irish citizenship in certain circumstances. He or she cannot be deprived of Irish citizenship acquired by birth or adoption. Citizenship may, however, be removed from a naturalised Irish citizen if the issue of the certificate of naturalisation was procured by fraud, misrepresentation, or concealment of material

facts or circumstances. Citizenship may also be removed if the person has been disloyal to the State or is a citizen of a country which is at war with the State. If a person, to whom a certificate of naturalisation has been granted, has been ordinarily resident outside the State for more than seven years without making a declaration of intention to retain Irish citizenship or if the person acquires another citizenship by a voluntary act other than marriage, citizenship may be removed.

138. The process of deprivation is overseen by a Committee of Inquiry appointed by the Minister for Justice under the terms of the Nationality and Citizenship Acts, 1956 and 1986. However, it should be emphasised that deprivation of citizenship is a very rare occurrence.

C.   Freedom of Expression (Art. 13)

139. Article 40.6.1 of the Constitution guarantees the rights of citizens, to express freely their convictions and opinions. This is subject only to provision for the law to deal with certain specified circumstances relating to public order and morality. So, for example, the Prohibition of Incitement to Hatred Act, 1989, makes it an offence to stir up hatred, whether orally, in writing or by any other means, against a group of persons in Ireland or any other country on account of their race, colour, nationality, religion, ethnic or national origins, membership of the Travelling Community or sexual orientation. This Act also makes it an offence to prepare or possess any material with a view to its being distributed, broadcast, or published in Ireland or any other country if the material is intended or likely to stir up such hatred.

D.   Access to Appropriate Information (Art.17)

140. Radio and television broadcasting services are provided by Radio Telefís Éireann (RTE) and independent radio stations operating under the Independent Radio and Television Commission (IRTC).

141. RTE is the national public service broadcaster established under the Broadcasting Authority Acts, 1960 to 1993. Under the legislation, RTE programming must be responsive to the needs of the whole community and have special regard for the varied elements of the culture of Ireland and in particular the Irish language.

142. In relation to the needs of children, RTE provides a range of information and entertainment programming, including Irish language content, mainly on weekday afternoons. At other times much of the programming is educational and entertaining for younger viewers.

143. The IRTC is responsible for arranging for the provision of sound broadcasting services and for the future establishment of a television service in addition to the services

provided by RTE. Radio stations operating under the auspices of the IRTC are local or community in nature. The IRTC has power to authorise the establishment of one independent national radio station. In awarding a radio franchise the IRTC has regard to the quality, range and type of programming to be provided, including programming in the Irish language. Due to the nature of the medium, sound broadcasting output is not primarily intended to appeal to children. In awarding the television franchise the IRTC would have regard to statutory obligations similar to those of RTE.

144. The Department of Social Welfare advertises its services on AERTEL (a form of teletext), which is a public information system available on RTE. Information officials from the Department regularly appear on public information programmes to advise on entitlements. The Department also administers information offices, staffed by specially trained officials in all parts of the country, where advice and information can be obtained. Such information is also available in the Irish language and in Braille or sign language.

Irish Language

145. The Irish language does not have a strong presence in the mass media. However, there has been strong support for the establishment of an all-Irish television service. The approval by Government of the establishment of such a service, Teilifís na Gaeilge represents an historic breakthrough in the provision of essential services for the people of the Gaeltacht and the Irish-speaking community nationwide.

146. An all-Irish radio station - Radio na Gaeltachta - based in the Gaeltacht is broadcast nationally and there is an all-Irish community radio station - Radio na Life - in Dublin. The publication of books and magazines in Irish is extremely lively and there is also a Sunday newspaper in Irish.

147. Bord na Leabhair Gaeilge (the Irish Language Books Board), has a policy of encouraging private publishers to produce books in Irish for both teenagers and younger children. In the years 1991 to 1994 inclusive, the Board supported a total of 47 books in these two categories. This represents 14.5% of all books grant-aided by the Board in that period. The work of the private publishers in this area complements the production of children's books by An Gum, and the educational material in book and other form produced by Comhar na Muinteoiri Gaeilge (Council of Teachers of Irish).

Public Library Service

148. Libraries are encouraged to devote a substantial proportion of their resources to children. In addition they undertake many activities and events specially for children. Where charges are in place, they are modified so as to encourage the full participation of children. Funding for new libraries is conditional on the provision of sufficient and suitable space and services for children in accordance with standards and guidelines set by An Chomhairle Leabharlanna (The Library Council).

Guidelines

149. RTE is aware of the possibility that certain types of broadcast material might not be suitable for children and operates a watershed of 9 p.m. in this regard. RTE operates guidelines in respect of the participation of children in general programmes, news and current affairs and in studio audiences. The portrayal of children in programmes is also covered by these guidelines.

Advertising

150. Codes of standards, practices and prohibitions in advertising on broadcast services drawn up by the Minister for Arts, Culture and the Gaeltacht impose specific restrictions on advertising near or during breaks in children's programming. Under the codes, advertisers are required to exert the utmost care and discretion in the transmission and presentation of such advertising. Advertisers may not exploit children's inexperience or credulity. They may not encourage minors to persuade their parents or others to purchase or make enquiries about goods or services being advertised. The Broadcasting Complaints Commission may investigate and decide on complaints of alleged breaches of the code by broadcasters.

151. The provisions of Article 22 of EU Directive 89/552/EEC, regarding programming which might seriously impair the physical, mental and moral development of children, have been given legal force in Irish law by way of statutory instrument.

Films

152. The Censorship of Films Acts, 1923 to 1992 provide that the Official Censor shall certify a picture as fit for exhibition in public unless the Censor is of the opinion that it is unfit by reason of being indecent, obscene or blasphemous, or because the exhibition would tend to inculcate principles contrary to public morality or would be otherwise subversive of public morality. However, the Censor may indicate that part only of a picture is unfit for exhibition, and may grant a certificate on removal of such part. The Censor may also grant a limited certificate, restricting viewing to certain classes of persons, generally by specifying that such persons must be above a certain age.

Videos

153. The Video Recordings Act, 1989 provides for the censorship of video works. The Official Censor may be of the opinion that a video work is unfit for exhibition in public if the viewing of it:

- would be likely to cause persons to commit crimes, whether by inciting or encouraging them to do so or by indicating or suggesting ways of doing so or of avoiding detection, or

- would be likely to stir up hatred against a group of persons in the State or elsewhere on account of their race, colour, nationality, religion, ethnic or national origins, membership of the Travelling Community or sexual orientation, or

- would tend, by reason of the inclusion in it of obscene or indecent matter, to deprave or corrupt persons who might view it, or

- it depicts acts of gross violence or cruelty (including mutilation and torture) towards humans or animals.

154.   A video recording may not be sold or rented unless the Official Censor has granted a supply certificate in respect of it. When granting a supply certificate, the Official Censor shall determine, and shall include in the certificate, a statement indicating to which of the following classes the video work belongs:

(a)   fit for viewing by persons generally

(b)   fit for viewing by persons generally but, in the case of a child under the age of 12 years, only in the company of a responsible adult,

(c)   fit for viewing by persons aged 15 years or more,

(d)   fit for viewing by persons aged 18 years or more.

Censorship of Publications.

155.   Censorship of publications in Ireland is governed by the Censorship of Publications Acts 1929 to 1967 (as amended by the Health (Family Planning) Act, 1979) and by the Censorship of Publications Regulations, 1980. The appointment of two boards is provided for under the Acts. They are the Censorship of Publications Board and the Censorship of Publications Appeal Board.

156.   The relevant procedures for making a complaint are set out in the regulations. The Board must have regard to the following in considering the complaint:

(a) the literary, artistic, scientific or historic merit or importance and the general tenor of the book;
(b) the language in which it is written;
(c) the nature and extent of the circulation which in their opinion it is likely to have;
(d) the class of reader which, in their opinion, may reasonably be expected to read it;
(e) any other matter relating to the book which appears to them to be relevant.

157. If the Board are of the opinion that a book is:

> (a) indecent or obscene, or

> (b) that it advocates the procurement of abortion or miscarriage or the use of any method, treatment or appliance for the purpose of such procurement,

they shall by order prohibit its sale and distribution.

158. When a book is the subject of a prohibition order the author, the editor, the publisher, or any five members of the Oireachtas acting jointly, may appeal the decision to the Censorship of Publications Appeal Board within twelve months of the prohibition order or twelve months after the date on which the prohibition order takes effect (whichever is later).

159. Periodical Publications can only be examined on receipt of a complaint. The board may then prohibit the publication if it is satisfied that recent issues thereof:-

> (a) have usually or frequently been indecent or obscene, or
> (b) have advocated the procurement of abortion or miscarriage or the use of any method, treatment or appliance for the purpose of such procurement, or
> (c) have devoted an unduly large proportion of space to the publication of matter relating to crime.

160. Where a periodical publication is the subject of a prohibition order, the Censorship of Publications Appeal Board, at any time on the application of the publisher, or the joint application of any five members of the Oireachtas, may revoke or vary the order so as to exclude from the application of the order any particular edition or issue of the periodical.

161. The Acts also provide for the keeping of a Register of Prohibited Publications and any member of the public may inspect the register free of charge. The register is in two parts, one relating to books and the other relating to periodical publications.

E. Freedom of Thought, Conscience and Religion (Art.14)

162. Article 44 of the Constitution provides as follows:

> "Freedom of conscience and the free profession and practice of religion are, subject to public order and morality, guaranteed to every citizen".

163. Article 42 of the Constitution grants parents the liberty to ensure that the religious and moral education of their children is fully protected. Article 42.1 reads as follows:

> "The State acknowledges that the primary and natural educator of the child is the family and guarantees to respect the inalienable right and duty of parents to provide, according to their means, for the religious and moral, intellectual, physical and social education of their children."

164. Most primary schools in Ireland receiving public funding are denominational in character. The Constitution permits the State to give financial assistance to denominational schools, and every child has the right to attend a denominational school receiving State funding without having to participate in religious instruction in the school.

165. In recent years, in response to local parental demand, a number of multi-denominational schools have been established. These schools receive State support in the same way as denominational schools.

166. Chaplains of different denominations are attached to prisons on a full time, part-time, or visiting basis as necessary. The Chaplain's main function is to make religious services available to offenders. Offenders participation is, of course, voluntary.

F. Freedom of Association and Peaceful Assembly (Art.15)

167. The Constitution guarantees the right to freedom of association. In Article 40.6.1, liberty for the exercise, subject to public order and morality, of, inter alia, "the right of citizens to form associations and unions" is guaranteed. The Article provides that laws may be enacted for the regulation and control in the public interest of the exercise of this right. Article 40.6.2 provides that laws regulating the manner in which the right of forming associations and unions may be exercised shall contain no political, religious or class discrimination. These rights apply equally to children and to adults.

168. Article 40.6.1 of the Constitution also guarantees the right of citizens to assemble peaceably and without arms, subject only to provision for the law to deal with certain specified circumstances relating to the protection of the public and the protection of the Houses of the Oireachtas (Parliament). So, for example, the Criminal Justice (Public Order) Act, 1994 provides for offences relating to disorderly conduct in public and threatening, abusive or insulting behaviour in public.

G. Protection of Privacy (Art. 16)

169. In addition to the large number of rights specified in the Constitution, Article 40.3.1 of the Constitution provides that the State guarantees in its laws to respect, and, as far as practicable, by its laws to defend and vindicate the personal rights of the citizen. The courts have recognised among these personal rights specific rights of privacy, including the right to privacy of communications, and this jurisprudence is open to further judicial development.

170.   As a general principle of criminal law, children enjoy the same degree of protection of privacy as adults. Searches by the Gardaí of private homes must be undertaken in accordance with the law. Interception of communications is regulated by law. There are also legal safeguards on the retention of personal information on computer.

H.   The Right not to be Subjected to Torture or Other Cruel, Inhuman or Degrading Treatment or Punishment (Art. 37 (a))

171.   Torture and cruel, inhuman or degrading treatment are contrary to the personal rights guaranteed to persons by Article 40.3 of the Constitution.

172.   In addition, regulations on the treatment of persons in Garda custody prohibit subjecting any person in custody to ill-treatment of any kind or the threat of ill-treatment, whether against the person, the person's family or any other person connected with him or her.

173.   Legislation is being prepared which will enable Ireland to ratify the UN Convention against Torture and other Cruel, Inhuman or Degrading Treatment or Punishment in the near future. Ireland signed this Convention on 28 September 1992. Ireland has signed and ratified the European Convention for the Prevention of Torture or Inhuman or Degrading Treatment or Punishment on 14 March 1988.

174.   Following a visit to Ireland in 1993 by a sub-committee of the Committee set up under the European Convention for the Prevention of Torture or Inhuman or Degrading Treatment or Punishment, the Committee's report on custodial arrangements applying in Ireland and the response of the Irish Government were published on 13 December 1995.

VI.   FAMILY ENVIRONMENT AND ALTERNATIVE CARE

A.   Parental Guidance (Art.5)

175.   An important principle informing the Child Care Act 1991 is that it is generally in the best interests of the child to be brought up in his or her own family. This reflects the constitutional guarantees protecting the family and respecting the rights of parents.

176.   The law as to guardianship and custody of children is governed by the Guardianship of Infants Act, 1964 (as amended by the Status of Children Act, 1987). The Act gives statutory expression to the equitable rule that all matters concerning guardianship and custody of children should be decided on the basis of the welfare of the child being regarded as the first and paramount consideration. Disputes between parents concerning children are usually determined under the 1964 Act. A child under the Act means a person under the age of 18 years.

177.   Married parents of a child are the guardians of that child jointly. In the case of unmarried parents, the mother is the guardian of the child. If the child's father subsequently marries the mother he automatically becomes a joint guardian; if not he has the right to apply to the Court to become a joint guardian.

178.   A parent who is a guardian has the power to appoint a guardian to act in the event of his/her death. The person so appointed acts jointly with the surviving parent. The courts have power to appoint a guardian in the interests of the child's welfare if a parent dies or if the appointed guardian refuses to act. A child ceases to be subject to guardianship when he or she reaches 18 years.

179.   In Ireland it is recognised that the promotion of parental involvement in the education of their children is an essential element of educational policy and practice. Parents associations have been established in individual primary and second-level schools in order to promote and develop effective participation by parents in education. The 1995 White Paper on Education proposes that parents will be given a statutory entitlement to representation on each school Board of Management and each Education Board.

B.   Parental Responsibilities (Art.18, paras. 1-2)

180.   A person who is a child's guardian has duties and rights in relation to all matters concerning the child's physical, intellectual, religious, social and moral welfare. Parents who are married to each other automatically hold equal rights as guardians until a child reaches the age of 18 years.

181.   Where parents separate, one may lose custody of a child by order of a court or by agreement. In such a case, the non-custodial parent remains a guardian and continues to be subject to duties, including the duty to maintain the child. The non-custodial guardian has the right to be made aware of, and consulted in relation to, major decisions and events affecting all aspects of the child's upbringing.

182.   Separation agreements usually, though not necessarily, contain detailed provisions relating to the custody of, and access to, children. A separation agreement is a binding legal contract enforceable in civil law. However, if either parent considers that the arrangements agreed upon are not working in the best interests of a child, he or she may apply to the Court for a custody or an access order or an order for a direction under section 11 of the Guardianship of Infants Act, 1964. In dealing with such an application the Court will take account of the agreement but will not be bound by its provisions. The welfare of the child is the first and paramount consideration and the Court's duty in considering the interests of the child transcends the agreement of the parents as to the custody of the child.

183.   Where parties cannot agree on the terms of their separation the Judicial Separation and Family Law Reform Act, 1989 empowers the Court to grant a decree of judicial separation and to make a variety of ancillary orders.

184.   The 1989 Act gives wide power to the Court to order support of a spouse and children in separation proceedings. It can order maintenance, lump sums, secured payments and redistribution of property including the family home, a business or any other property.

185.   The Act provides that a Court may not grant a decree of judicial separation, where there is a dependent child of the family, unless either it is satisfied that proper provision has been made for the child's welfare or, by order, intends upon the granting of the decree to make provision for the child's welfare. It also provides that, on granting a decree of judicial separation, the Court must, in considering the matter of occupancy or sale of the family home, have regard to the welfare of the family as a whole and to the fact that it may not be possible for the spouses to continue residing together. Where the parties cannot reach agreement on the terms of separation the Court is allowed to make orders on the basis of all the evidence before it in each case with particular reference to what is best for any children of the family.

186.   The Court may declare, upon granting a judicial separation, that either spouse is unfit to have custody of a child and is not automatically entitled to custody on the death of the other spouse.

187.   Parties to judicial separation proceedings are encouraged to consider alternatives to such proceedings. Parties must be informed by their legal representatives about the possibilities of reconciliation (and the use of counselling for that purpose) or of mediation, to help effect a separation involving agreed arrangements in respect of the children, the family home and other assets.

C.   **Separation from Parents (Art. 9)**

188.   Under the Child Care Act, 1991 the Health Boards are empowered to provide assistance to parents in the upbringing of their children to help make it possible for children to grow up in their own families, even in adverse circumstances. Each of the

eight Health Boards are developing child and family support services which aim to promote the welfare of children in vulnerable families and to limit the circumstances by which a child may have to be received into the care of a Health Board. Only in exceptional cases is a child taken into care. A child can be taken into care on a voluntary basis, with the agreement of the parent(s) or guardian. However, the law provides for the taking into care of a child without the consent of the parents, where the parents have neglected or ill-treated the child or where there are other compelling reasons why the welfare of the child demands that it be removed from its family.

Children in Care of Health Boards at 31/12/1992	
Children placed in Foster Care	2,284
Children placed in Residential Care	765
Other types of Care	41
Total number of Children in Care	3,090

Age of Children in Care in 1992							
<I year	1-2 years	2-4 years	4-7 years	7-12 years	12-16 years	>16 years	Total
94	89	216	385	927	849	530	3090

189.   The provisions in the Child Care Act, 1991 update the powers of the Courts and the Health Boards to act in the interests of the welfare of a child, while incorporating important checks and balances in terms of the rights of the natural parents. Under the Child Care Act a child may be taken into compulsory care under the following orders:

● **An Emergency Care Order** (replacing the Place of Safety Order in the Children Act 1908) will place the child in question under the care of the Health Board for any period up to a maximum of eight days, where there is reasonable cause to believe that there is an immediate and serious risk to the child's safety which necessitates placement in care.

● **A Care Order** commits a child to the care of a Health Board until his or her eighteenth birthday, or for some shorter period as determined by the court. A care order may be made where the Court is satisfied that:

(a)   the child has been or is being assaulted, ill-treated, neglected or sexually abused or

(b)   the child's health, development or welfare has been or is being avoidably impaired or neglected, or

(c)   the child's health, development or welfare is likely to be avoidably impaired or neglected.

* **An Interim Care Order** may be made placing a child in the care of a Health Board until a decision is reached on an application for a care order. This is designed to "bridge the gap" between the expiration of an emergency care order and the determination of an application for a full care order. An interim care order may be made for 8 days or, if the parents consent, for longer than 8 days and may be renewed from time to time.

190.   Apart from the provisions of the Child Care Act, the courts may also commit children to special residential schools in response to persistent school non attendance or the commission of offences.

Supervision Order

191.   A Supervision Order may be made where a court is satisfied that there are reasonable grounds for believing that any of the conditions for a care order are fulfilled. The Supervision Order allows the Health Board to have the child visited and inspected at home and to give the necessary advice to the parents. The order may also require the parents to cause the child to attend for medical or psychiatric examination, treatment or assessment at a hospital, clinic or other place specified by the court. The Act gives parents a right of appeal where they are dissatisfied with the nature of the board's supervision.

192.   Where children must live apart from their parents for good reason there is still a strong commitment to preserving where at all possible, a meaningful role for the family. Section 37 of the Child Care Act 1991 requires the Health Boards to facilitate reasonable access to a child in its care, whether on a voluntary or compulsory basis, to a parent, someone acting in loco parentis or to any person whom the Board considers to have a bona fide interest in the child. Any person dissatisfied with access arrangements can seek a court ruling under this section. Health Boards may, however, seek a court order denying this facility to a named person.

Persons in Garda Custody

193.   For arrested persons in Garda custody, regulations require the Gardaí to give information to any person who makes an enquiry as to the Garda station where the person is in custody, provided the person in custody consents to this and the release of the information does not hinder or delay the investigation of a crime. Where the arrested person is under 17 years, a parent or guardian must be informed of the fact that the person is in custody in the Garda station, of the reason for the arrest and of

the right to consult a solicitor. The parent or guardian is also required to attend at the Garda station without delay.

194. In the case of prisoners under the age of 18 years, the draft new Prison Rules (see paragraph 540) provides for the Governor to take particular care to inform the parent(s), or any other person acting in loco parentis, of the prison in which they are detained.

D. Family Reunification (Art. 10)

195. Applications for family reunion are treated humanely and are dealt with as expeditiously as possible. Where a person is legally resident in Ireland, the administrative policy is to allow any dependent unmarried children to join that parent in Ireland. It is proposed to put this policy on a legislative basis in relation to persons granted refugee status.

196. In addition to the obligations which arise for Ireland under the 1956 Geneva convention and the 1967 Protocol to that Convention in respect of individual asylum seekers, the Government operate two on-going refugee resettlement programmes.

197. These programmes allow for the admission to Ireland of groups of people who have fled their country of origin or normal residence because their lives, freedom or safety are threatened by violence or conflict. Decisions to admit groups of people from conflict situations for resettlement are taken by the Government on the advice of the Minister of Foreign Affairs. All Government decisions on the admission of such groups place particular importance on family reunification. In any decision to admit a group of refugees, provision is made to enable certain close relatives to join their family later.

198. Two refugee resettlement programmes are currently operated for Bosnian and Vietnamese nationals pursuant to Government decisions. There are currently 557 Vietnamese refugees in Ireland, including 145 children born in Ireland and there are 540 Bosnian refugees, in Ireland including 24 children born in Ireland. All the individuals covered by these two refugee resettlement programmes have access to health, education, employment and social services on the same basis as Irish citizens. See also Paragraphs 525-535 on this issue.

E. Recovery of Maintenance for the Child (Art. 27, para. 4)

199. The Guardianship of Infants Act, 1964 confers powers on the Courts to order the father or mother of a child to pay money towards the maintenance of the child. The Family Law Maintenance of Spouses and Children Act, 1976 provides that failure to maintain is the basis for either spouse to seek maintenance.

200.   The 1976 Act empowers the Court to order the respondent, on application to it by his or her spouse, to make periodic payments (i.e. weekly, monthly etc.) for the maintenance of the applicant spouse or children. A lump sum order not exceeding IR£750 may be granted in respect of the birth of a child or in respect of the funeral expenses of a child.

201.   A Court is also empowered under the Act to direct that periodic payments under an order are to be made through the District Court Clerk and authorises the Clerk to initiate such proceedings as he considers necessary to secure the payment of any arrears that arise.

202.   The obligation to maintain a child ceases when the child reaches the age of 16 years or the age of 21 years if the child is in full-time education. The Family Law Act , 1994 increases the 21 years provision to 23 years. In addition it empowers the Court to grant a lump sum order in lieu of a periodic payments order or in addition to such an order.

203.   The Status of Children Act, 1987, equalises the right to maintenance of marital and non-marital children. Section 5A of the 1976 Act (as inserted by section 18 of the 1987 Act) provides that maintenance orders may be granted against either the father or the mother of a non-marital child.

204.   Section 15 of the 1987 Act provides that where the question of parentage is at issue, the Court shall determine such parentage on the common law doctrine of the balance of probabilities.

205.   Where parents enter into an agreement in writing which provides for the making of periodic payments by one parent to the other for the maintenance of the child, the High Court or Circuit Court may, if it is satisfied that such agreement is fair and reasonable, make an order making the agreement a rule of Court. The agreement then becomes enforceable as if it were a Court order granted under the 1976 Act.

206.   The Judicial Separation and Family Law Reform Act, 1989, provides - upon the granting of a judicial separation - for the making by one spouse of periodical payments (secured or unsecured), lump sum payments and property transfer or sale orders for the benefit of, inter alia, a dependent child.

207.   The Family Law Act 1994, strengthens the enforcement powers of the Courts in relation to maintenance generally by providing, subject to certain conditions, for automatic attachment of earnings without the need to prove default in complying with a Court order. It also gives the Courts power to order lump sum payments for the support of children in all proceedings affecting child maintenance.

208.   The Maintenance Orders Act, 1974 gave effect to an agreement on the reciprocal recognition and enforcement of periodic maintenance orders between the State and the United Kingdom. In addition, public officials in both Ireland and the United Kingdom

provide free administrative assistance to a maintenance creditor in either jurisdiction who wishes to avail of the provisions of the agreement.

209.   Separate provision is made under the Social Welfare legislation for the "liability to maintain family". The relevant sections in the Social Welfare Consolidation Act, 1993, are Sections 286(1) and 298(1).

210.   These provisions are based on the widely accepted obligation on people to maintain their spouses and children. Under the legislation, where a marriage breakdown occurs and a family is dependent on a Social Welfare payment, the person who is liable to maintain that family must contribute to the Department towards the cost of the family's income support, with due regard to their financial situation and a determination of their ability to contribute. Liable relatives pay either by way of regular direct contribution to the Department of Social Welfare or through family law court orders which are transferred to the Department. The Department of Social Welfare may take legal proceedings where the liable relative has failed to comply with the legislation.

211.   The Irish social security system is being changed to ensure that no person will be disadvantaged in terms of social security entitlements as a result of a change in their legal status from married, deserted or separated to divorced.

212.   The Jurisdiction of Courts and Enforcement of Judgements (European Communities) Act, 1988, facilitated Ireland's accession to the Brussels Convention on Jurisdiction and Enforcement of Judgments in Civil and Commercial Matters, 1968. This Convention provides, inter alia, for the mutual enforcement of maintenance orders throughout the European Community. The Jurisdiction of Courts and Enforcement of Judgements Act, 1993 allowed Ireland to accede to a similar convention between EU and EFTA States. Unlike the 1974 agreement, however, no administrative assistance is provided for.

213.   The Maintenance Act, 1994 enables Ireland to ratify two international conventions (the Rome Convention of 1990 and the New York Convention of 1956), both of which provide administrative assistance to maintenance creditors who wish to recover maintenance from maintenance debtors who reside in over forty countries worldwide (including EU and EFTA countries). Arrangements are being made to have both Conventions ratified by the State.

F.   **Children Deprived of a Family Environment (Art.20)**

214.   Care can be provided by placing the child with a foster parent, in residential care or in the case of an eligible child, with a suitable person with a view to adoption, or by other suitable arrangements (including placement with a relative) as may be made by the Health Board. For information on regulations governing the placement of children in residential care, foster care or with relatives see paragraphs 102 and 103.

215. Section 38 of the Act requires the Health Boards to ensure that there is an adequate number of residential places available in its area to cater for children in need of care or who are likely to come into care. In fulfilling its obligations, Health Boards are given the freedom to provide these residential places themselves or to do so by arrangement with voluntary non-governmental bodies.

216. Section 61 of the Child Care Act (to be implemented in 1996) provides for a scheme of registration of children's residential centres. When this scheme is in operation it will be unlawful for persons to offer residential child care services unless they have been registered by their Health Board.

217. Regulations under section 63 of the Act will set down the standards for children's residential centres in relation to adequate and suitable accommodation, food and care for children and the proper conduct of these centres. Each Health Board will be responsible for ensuring that the standards of care in children's residential centres operated by voluntary bodies in its area are acceptable. The Minister for Health will regulate and inspect residential care services run by the Health Boards.

218. Pending the implementation of regulations under section 63, a Draft Guide to Standards in Children's Residential centres has been prepared and has been circulated to the various interest groups for their views. When completed, this Guide will advise all agencies concerned with residential care for children on the standards that should obtain in such centres. See also paragraph 121.

Domestic Violence

219. The Department of Health, through the Health Boards, supports refuges and other services for victims of domestic violence. There are currently a total of 16 centres in Ireland providing emergency accommodation for victims of domestic violence - women and children. The level of financial support provided by the Health Boards to women's refuges nationally represents almost 90% of the refuges total expenditure.

220. The Government accepts that the current level of provision for victims of domestic violence is inadequate. The Governments recent published discussion document **"Developing a Policy for Women's Health"** has identified services available to women who are victims of domestic violence as a priority area for development. Additional resources are being made available to increase the availability of refuge accommodation and other support services.

Homeless Children

221. Section 5 of the Child Care Act, which is in operation since 1 October 1992, imposes a statutory duty on Health Boards to investigate the circumstances of homeless children and, in appropriate cases, either to receive such children into care or to take steps to provide accommodation for such children up to 18 years. In preparation for

the implementation of this provision, special funding was made available in 1991 and 1992 for the development of new services and facilities for homeless children

222.   The problem of homeless young people has been recognised and is being actively addressed by all Health Boards through the provision of hostel accommodation and other services. During 1993 additional hostel places were provided as part of a package of new child care developments which were approved for each Health Board area. The Child Care Action Plans, 1994 and 1995 also provided for the development of new services for the young homeless

223.   A report commissioned by the Eastern Health Board, which covers one third of the population (including Dublin City), in association with voluntary organisations ascertained that 429 young people had presented as homeless during 1994. The Eastern Health Board, which has the responsibility for the administration of child care and family support services in that area, has established a day centre and drop-in service for the young homeless in Dublin. This provides young persons out of home with a daytime facility and direct contact with the service providers. It can also serve to alert the professionals concerned to children who might not otherwise come to their attention.

224.   The Board has also established an emergency/short term care facility which can cater for up to 14 young people who are temporarily out of home or are awaiting a more long term placement. This development greatly strengthens the capacity of the Eastern Health Board to provide appropriate accommodation and services for homeless young people and should help to minimise the use of bed and breakfast accommodation for this purpose, a response which is generally regarded as inappropriate in such circumstances.

Aftercare

225.   Section 45 of the Child Care Act empowers Health Boards to provide assistance to young people who leave care until they reach 21 years of age, or beyond that age until the completion of full-time education. Such aftercare may take the form of continuous monitoring by a Health Board, arranging for the completion of a young person's education, by contributing towards maintenance, or by placing him or her in a suitable trade, calling or business and paying such fee or sum as may be required for that purpose, or by co-operating with housing authorities in planning accommodation for children leaving care on reaching the age of 18 years.

G.   Adoption (Art.21)

226.   Ireland operates a system of full adoption (adoptio plena). On the making of an adoption order a natural parent(s) loses all legal rights over the child and is freed from all duties. These rights and duties are transferred to the adoptive parents. The child is regarded in law as the child of the adoptive parents as if he/she were born to them in marriage. Legal adoption is permanent.

227.   The position of adoption in Irish Law is governed and controlled by the Adoption Acts 1952-1991. Adoption Societies registered under the Adoption Act 1952, and the Health Boards, are the only agencies legally entitled to place children for adoption. Adoption Societies are supervised by the Adoption Board with which they are required to be registered.

228.   All applications for adoption orders are made to the **Adoption Board,** an independent quasi-judicial body. The Board consists of a chairman and eight ordinary members appointed by the Government. The primary function of the Board is to grant or refuse applications for adoption orders. Under section 9 of the Adoption Act, 1952 the power to make an adoption order is vested solely in the Adoption Board. It also has the responsibility for registering and supervising the adoption societies and for regulating and recognising foreign adoptions.

229.   A child being considered for adoption must reside in the State, be at least six weeks old and under 18 years of age. The child need not have been born in this country.

Birth Place of Children		
	1993	**1994**
Urban	319	261
Rural	143	132
Outside State	38	31
TOTAL	500	424

230.   The principle that the child is the most important person in the adoption process is fully embodied in the law. The legislation requires the Adoption Board, or any Court, when dealing with any matter relating to an adoption, to regard the welfare of the child as the first and paramount consideration.

231.   The Adoption Acts also make provision for the wishes of the child to be taken into account, where a child is more than seven years of age at the date of the application for the adoption order.

232.   The majority of adoptable children are born outside marriage and the consent of the natural mother only is all that is normally required. However, the consent of the natural father is required where he marries the natural mother after the birth of a child and the birth of the child is subsequently re-registered or he is appointed a guardian of the child or is granted custody of the child pursuant to a court order or otherwise.

Adoption Orders made		
	1993	**1994**
Boys	266	212
Girls	234	212
TOTAL	500	424

233.   A child born to a married woman but whose husband is not the father, is eligible for adoption provided the facts of the child's paternity can be proven to the satisfaction of the Adoption Board.

234.   The law permits the adoption of orphans and children born outside marriage, including, in certain circumstances, children whose natural parents subsequently marry each other. A child born outside marriage whose natural parents subsequently marry is eligible for adoption provided his/her birth has not been re-registered.

235.   The consent of every person being a guardian of a child or having charge of, or control over, a child, is normally required to the placing of a child for adoption and to the making of an adoption order for a child.

Keegan Judgement

236.   Except in the circumstances related at paragraph 232 above, however, the consent of the father of a child born outside marriage is not required at present in order to effect a valid adoption, nor is the father a person entitled to be heard in the adoption process. However, in 1994 the European Court of Human Rights found Ireland to be in breach of the Convention for the Protection of Human Rights and Fundamental Freedoms in allowing a child born outside marriage to be placed by the natural mother for adoption without the father's knowledge or consent.

237.   In its judgement in the case **Keegan -v- Ireland**, the Court held that the essential problem with existing Irish adoption law is that it permits the secret placement for adoption of a child born outside marriage without the knowledge or consent of the child's father.

238.   The Department of Health, in consultation with the Office of the Attorney General, has been examining the implications of this judgement for Irish adoption law and procedures. An appropriate legislative response to the issues raised in the judgement is in the course of preparation.

Consent

239.   Consent to the making of an adoption order may not be given until the child is at least six weeks old and may be withdrawn at any time before the making of the adoption

order by the Adoption Board. The Adoption Board makes the adoption order after consent is given by the parents to the adoption.

240.   The Adoption Board must satisfy itself that every person who has given consent to the making of an adoption order understands the nature and effect of the consent, of the adoption order and of certain legal rights. In order to comply with this requirement, the Board appoints authorised persons to interview the consenting party on its behalf.

241.   The Board may dispense with the requirement for consent if it is satisfied that the person whose consent is required is incapable by reason of mental infirmity of giving consent or cannot be found.

242.   Where the consenting party fails, neglects or refuses to give consent to the making of an adoption order, or withdraws a consent already given, it is open to the adopting parents, if they have applied for an adoption order for the child, to apply to the High Court for an order under section 3 of the Adoption Act, 1974. The High Court, if it is satisfied that it is in the best interests of the child to do so, may make an order under that section giving custody of the child to the adopting parents for a specified period and authorising the Adoption Board to dispense with the necessary consent to the making of an adoption order.

243.   On the other hand, where a natural mother changes her mind about adoption before the making of the adoption order and seeks to reclaim her child but the adopting parents refuse to give up the child, then it is open to the natural mother to institute legal proceedings to have custody of the child restored to her.

244.   In exceptional cases, the High Court may make orders under section 3 of the Adoption Act, 1988 authorising the adoption of children whose parents have failed in their constitutional duty towards them. Consent is not required to the adoption of a child who is the subject of such an order. Children born within marriage may be adopted under this provision.

Post-Adoption Contact

245.   Because of the confidential nature of adoption proceedings, access to adoption records, including birth records of adopted persons is restricted. An order of the adoption board or of a Court is necessary and the test "the best interests of the child" is applied to an application for such an order. Where a request is made by a child for information regarding the child's natural mother the Adoption Board must consider each application on its merits. The Board may only release such information in a case where it is satisfied that it is appropriate and proper to do so and where it is satisfied that it is in the best interests of the child to do so.

246.   The legal adoption system has evolved on the basis of confidentiality. The Adoption Board and the adoption agencies will not consider disclosing identifying information about a party to adoption without first endeavouring to obtain the current consent of

that person. Adopted persons do not have a right of access to their original birth records and they are dependent on the co-operation of agencies in their search for information.

247. In the light of recent developments in adoption practice and the changing nature of adoptions, the Health Strategy contains a commitment to introduce changes in adoption law and procedure to provide for arrangements to facilitate contact between adopted persons and their natural parent/s. The question of an adopted person's right of access to his/her original birth certificate will be considered in that context.

Intercountry Adoption

248. The Adoption Act, 1991, sets out statutory procedures for the recognition of certain adoptions effected outside the State. The legislation contains a definition of a foreign adoption and only adoptions which comply with the terms of the definition are entitled to recognition.

249. Among the main features of the definition is the requirement that the foreign adoption must be effected in accordance with the law of the foreign country concerned. Furthermore the adopted person must be under the age of 18 years at the date of the adoption, or, if the adoption was effected before 30 May 1991, under the age of 21 years.

250. The foreign adoption must have also essentially the same legal effect as an Irish adoption order in relation to the termination and creation of parental rights and duties and the adopters must not have made or received any improper payments in consideration of the adoption.

251. The legislation also provides for the recognition of a foreign adoption effected in favour of a person or a married couple who at the date of the adoption were domiciled or habitually resident in the foreign country or were ordinarily resident there for at least one year immediately preceding the date of the adoption.

252. The legislation also provides for the recognition of a foreign adoption effected in a country other than the adopter's country of domicile, habitual residence or ordinary residence in any case where the adoption is recognised under the law of the latter country.

253. The 1991 Act lays down separate procedures for the recognition of adoptions effected abroad in favour of Irish residents. Special transitional arrangements apply to such adoptions which were effected before the enactment of the legislation. Broadly speaking, such an adoption qualifies for recognition provided the adopters satisfy the legal eligibility criteria to adopt under Irish law and the adoption complies with the terms of the definition of a foreign adoption referred to above.

254.   Since the enactment of the legislation, Irish residents wishing to adopt children abroad must have their eligibility and suitability to adopt formally established in advance in order for such foreign adoptions to qualify for recognition. This adoption assessment, which must be undertaken by an adoption agency and approved by the Adoption Board, provides an important protection for the welfare of the child and ensures that children concerned in inter-country adoptions enjoy safeguards and standards equivalent to those existing in the case of national adoptions. This approach is in compliance with the Convention on the Rights of the Child.

255.   Under the terms of the Adoption Act, 1991 recognition of the adoption is withheld in any case where the adopters made or received improper payments or any other reward in consideration of the foreign adoption.

256.   In 1993, 59 foreign adoptions were recognised and entered in the Register of Foreign Adoptions while in 1994, 64 foreign adoptions were recognised and entered in the Register of Foreign Adoptions.

Bilateral Adoption Agreements

257.   The objectives of Article 21 are a central feature of the bilateral adoption agreement between Ireland and Romania which was finalised in July 1994. The possibility of entering into similar accords with certain other countries is currently being explored.

The Hague Convention

258.   Ireland participated in the preparation of the Hague Convention on Protection of Children and Co-Operation in respect of Intercountry Adoption which was completed in May 1993. This Convention takes account of the principles set forth in the Convention on the Rights of the Child. The National Health Strategy contains a commitment to amend current domestic law relating to foreign adoptions so as to enable the Hague Convention to be ratified. Ireland will shortly sign the Hague Convention on Inter-Country Adoption an will ratify when the necessary legislative measures are in place.

H.   Illicit Transfer and Non-return (Art.11)

259.   The Child Abduction and Enforcement of Custody Orders Act, 1991 deals with problems that arise when a person abducts a child (under the age of 16 years) across international frontiers in defiance of a Court order or against the wishes of a parent or guardian with custody rights. It primarily deals with child abduction by one parent against the wishes of another.

260.   The Act gives the force of law in Ireland to two international conventions - the Hague Convention on the Civil Aspects of International Child Abduction and the

Luxembourg Convention on Recognition and Enforcement of Decisions concerning Custody of Children and on Restoration of Custody of Children.

261.   Both Conventions require the establishment of a Central Authority in contracting states. The Minister for Equality and Law Reform is designated as the Central Authority for both Conventions. The Conventions have proved to be of substantial benefit. In 1994, the Irish Central Authority dealt with 112 child abduction cases, 55 involving children who had been abducted into the State and 57 involving children who had been abducted from the State.

262.   When a foreign application for the return of a child is received in Ireland it is generally referred by the Irish Central Authority to the Legal Aid Board for relevant proceedings to be taken before the High Court. Foreign applicants under both Conventions are entitled to free legal aid in Ireland irrespective of means and the Central Authority itself imposes no charge for its services.

263.   Section 37 of the Act gives the Gardaí power to detain a child whom they reasonably suspect is being removed from the State in breach of any custody order (including orders made under either Convention) or while proceedings in relation to custody orders are pending or about to be made.

I.   Abuse and Neglect (Art. 19), including Physical and Psychological Recovery and Social Reintegration (Art.39)

264.   In Ireland child abuse is now recognised as a significant social problem. In 1986 the number of reports of alleged child abuse received by the Health Boards was just over 1000. In almost 500 of these cases the abuse was confirmed, including 247 cases of child sexual abuse. The latest available figures indicate that Health Boards are now receiving almost 5,000 reports of alleged abuse each year, of which about 1,500 cases are confirmed, including about 600 cases of sexual abuse. Reports of cases of physical and sexual abuse and neglect have been reported extensively in the media and have given rise to considerable public disquiet.

Kilkenny Report

265.   A Government inquiry was set up in the wake of what is known as the "Kilkenny Case" which became the focal point for a complete re-evaluation of social attitudes to child abuse. The case concerned a young woman who had suffered horrific abuse at the hands of her father for many years. She had suffered serious sexual and physical assaults as a result of which she lost the sight in one eye. Questions were asked by many commentators about the apparent failure of the appropriate social services to respond and assist when the matter came to their attention.

266.   Following the conviction of the man responsible for the abuse, the Government set up an Inquiry under the aegis of the South Eastern Health Board. This inquiry was

chaired by the then Senior Counsel, Catherine McGuinness now a Judge of the Circuit Court. The findings of the **Kilkenny Report** were published and provoked widespread debate. The findings and recommendations have provided a reference point for all professionals working in the area of child care. Many of the recommendations in this report have already been implemented or are being carefully considered with a view to implementation, subject to legal and constitutional requirements. In some instances they consist of new initiatives while in other areas procedures and guidelines already in place have been refined and strengthened.

Response to Report

267. The Government has set out to provide as much assistance as it can to deal with the problem. The measures being taken cannot guarantee complete prevention of child abuse but they can contribute to improving concrete protection for children.

268. The principal step is the full implementation of the Child Care Act, 1991. The Government has set the target date of 31 December 1996 for the complete implementation of the Act which is being introduced on a phased basis. This is due to the requirement that the necessary resources be provided and the mechanisms put in place before it is fully implemented. As resources and trained personnel come on stream the relevant sections of the Act are then brought into legal effect by Ministerial order. The full implementation of this Act is in line with the recommendations of the Kilkenny Report.

269. The Child Care Act provides a statutory framework for the development of child care services, including tackling the problem of child abuse. The Act imposes a statutory duty on Health Boards to identify children who are not receiving adequate care and protection, including children who have suffered abuse, and requires them to provide a range of child care and family support services. Parts III to VI of the Act were brought into operation on 31 October 1995. These deal with the protection of children in emergencies, care proceedings and the powers and duties of Health Boards in relation to children in their care. They strengthen the powers of the Gardaí, Health Boards and the courts to intervene and protect children who are being abused or neglected.

Abuse Prevention Guidelines

270. The 1987 Child Abuse Guidelines, issued by the Department of Health, provide guidance generally for personnel working with children, and in particular for health and social service agencies, on the identification, investigation and management of child abuse. Responsibility for monitoring and co-ordinating the management of such cases rests with the Health Boards as part of the child care services within the community care programme.

271. A number of Health Boards have expanded the Guidelines (circulated by the Department of Health) and produced their own local Child Protection Guidelines, following consultation with interested bodies in their area.

272. Additional procedures have been developed in order to clarify the circumstances in which suspected cases of child abuse should be notified between the Health Boards and the Gardaí and to provide a uniform framework for dealing with such cases. The primary objective of the procedures is to ensure closer co-ordination between the Gardaí and the Health Boards in the investigation and management of suspected cases of abuse so as to facilitate the twin objectives of protecting the child and the full investigation of any crime.

273. The Department of Education issued guidelines to all primary schools in November 1991 under the title "Procedures for dealing with Allegations of Child Abuse", and to Post Primary schools in 1992, under the title "Procedures for Dealing with Allegations or Suspicions of Child Abuse". The guidelines were drawn up in consultation with the "Partners in Education", i.e. the parents, teachers, school managements, and other interested parties. These guidelines set down the procedures to be followed in the event of allegations or suspicions of child abuse.

274. Special units for the investigation and management of alleged child sexual abuse are in operation in the major centres of population around the country. Each Health Board has services in place for the treatment and support of victims of child abuse, some of which are hospital-based while others are provided at a community level. Special funding has been made available to the Health Boards for the expansion of these services.

275. A provision in the Criminal Law (Sexual Offences) Act, 1993 fully implemented the recommendation of the Kilkenny Report relating to the protection of mentally handicapped persons. This amended the law relating to sexual intercourse with the mentally handicapped.

276. In drafting new legislation in this area the Department of Equality and Law Reform has addressed the question of extending the legislation for barring spouses, to cohabitants. This can be seen in the provisions of the Domestic Violence Bill, 1995. For further details see Paragraph 285.

277. A treatment programme for sex offenders is in operation in the Central Mental Hospital and in Arbour Hill prison. In Dublin, the Northside Inter-Agency project, which is composed of staff from The Children's Hospital Temple Street, the Mater Hospital and the Eastern Health Board, operates a treatment programme for adolescent abusers. This programme is based on a group work model and requires the active involvement of parents. A research project is being undertaken by the Northside Inter-Agency Project into therapeutic programmes for male adolescent sex offenders. The Department of Health has confirmed that a grant of IR£10,000 will be provided to fund the project which will examine the outcomes of a recently completed 5 year

programme for male adolescent sex offenders. Also in Dublin, Our Lady's Hospital for Sick Children intends to develop a programme aimed at adolescent perpetrators of child sexual abuse. Programmes for adult perpetrators of sexual abuse have been developed by some Health Boards.

278.   There is currently a liaison arrangement in place between the Social Services authorities in Ireland and the UK on child protection matters. New procedures have been put in place to ensure exchange of information between the Health Boards in this jurisdiction and the authorities in Northern Ireland in relation to children at risk whose families move between both jurisdictions.

279.   Within the Garda Síochána, a Domestic Violence and Sexual Assault Investigation Unit was established in 1993. The Unit is staffed by Gardaí who are highly trained and experienced in dealing with domestic violence, child sexual abuse and other violent and sexual offences committed against women and children. The unit also liaises with organisations, both statutory and voluntary, which deal with these crimes. In addition to the work of this Unit, it is Garda policy that all members of the Force should be able to investigate violent and sexual crimes against women and children. These issues form an integral part of training for all new Garda recruits, involving a three day course on the social, psychological and legal aspects of such crimes. Existing members of the Force are updated with the latest investigative techniques through the in-service training programme.

Garda Clearance of Applicants for Posts in Children's Residential Centres

280.   The procedures for the recruitment and selection of staff to children's residential centres were revamped during 1994. Candidates for posts must make a written declaration with their application stating that there are no criminal convictions recorded against them or provide details of any convictions recorded against them as the case may be. In addition to this declaration, candidates shall be required to sign an authorization to enable the details given to be verified with the Garda authorities. Checks are then carried out with the local Gardaí to establish if the person in question has a criminal background. This criterion came into operation in November 1994 and each children's residential centre was issued with detailed guidelines outlining the appropriate procedures to be followed. Further directions were issued by the Department of Health to each Health Board in September 1995 outlining new vetting procedures to be followed in the recruitment and selection of staff to any area of the health service where they would have access to children or vulnerable individuals

Foster Care

281.   The Child Care (Placement of Children in Foster Care) Regulations 1995 require Health Boards to have children placed in foster care visited regularly in order to ensure their safety and welfare. A similar requirement is imposed on the Health Boards under the Child Care (Placement of Children in Residential Care) Regulations 1995 and the Child Care (Placement of Children with Relatives) Regulations 1995 .

Child Abuse Prevention

282. Following discussions between the Departments of Health and Education and the Irish National Teachers Organisation, the National Parents Council and school managerial bodies, a "Stay Safe" Child Abuse Prevention Programme was designed for use in primary schools.

283. The programme consists of a video for children, two separate curricula for junior and senior cycles, a training course for teachers and additional information for parents. Before the programme is launched in a school, the parents are consulted. The aim of the programme is to prevent all forms of child abuse by equipping parents and teachers with the knowledge and skills necessary to protect the children in their care. Children are taught safety skills in the normal classroom context and these skills are reinforced through discussion with their parents.

284. A similar programme is being drawn up for second level schools. This is most likely to be achieved by incorporating the principles of the Stay Safe programme into the programme in Relationships and Sexuality Education. (see Par 370).

Domestic Violence

285. The most widely used remedy in the area of domestic violence is a civil law barring order. That remedy was introduced by section 22 of the Family Law (Maintenance of Spouses and Children) Act, 1976. The court was empowered, on the application of the spouse, to bar the respondent spouse from entering any place where the applicant spouse or a dependent child resided if there were reasonable grounds for believing that the safety or welfare of the applicant spouse or child so required. The maximum duration of an order granted by the District Court was three months.

286. The Family Law (Protection of Spouses and Children) Act 1981 strengthened the law on barring orders. The main changes made by the Act were the extension of the District Court's time limit from 3 months to 12 months, the creation of a new type of order, called a protection order, and the granting of statutory powers of arrest to the Gardaí for breaches of barring and protection orders. Protection orders are designed to provide immediate protection for the applicant spouse or child pending the determination of the barring order application. They fall short of barring the offending spouse from the family home.

287. On or after an application for a decree of judicial separation, the court may grant a barring order or a protection order and the court may confer on one spouse the right to occupy the family home subject to such conditions as it thinks proper, or it may transfer ownership of the home to either spouse in suitable cases.

288. The law in relation to the protection of victims of domestic violence has been subjected to scrutiny in major Government-sponsored reports such as the "Kilkenny

Report". These reports advocate the extension of the legislation to cover cohabitants and their children and the more widespread availability of protection orders, not as an interim measure pending the granting of a barring order as at present, but as an alternative remedy in its own right. The reports pointed to the lack of support available to victims who were faced with the trauma of having to seek protection and recommended that outside agencies such as Health Boards or Gardaí should be given a role in such cases.

289.   The Domestic Violence Bill, 1995, currently before the Oireachtas, seeks to extend the law on "barring orders" and "protection orders" (at present confined to spouses and their children) to other categories of persons including cohabitants and their children; it gives the Health Boards new powers, subject to conditions, to apply to the court for orders under the Bill; it increases the penalties for breaches of orders of the court; and it gives the Gardaí new powers of arrest to deal with cases of domestic violence.

Children Begging

290.   The problem of children begging relates mainly to the Dublin city centre area and primarily involves children of the Travelling Community. The number of children involved is generally small but can vary depending on the time of year, with Christmas and the summer holidays being the peak periods. The children come from a small number of families. While it is a criminal offence for parents to send their children to beg, the Gardaí face considerable difficulties in taking prosecutions because of the need to prove that the parents sent the children out to beg. The need to strengthen the law in this regard is being examined in the context of the preparation of legislation to replace the Children Act, 1908.

J.   Periodic Review of Placement (Art. 25)

291.   In accordance with article 25 of the Convention, section 42 of the Child Care Act 1991 makes provision for the Minister for Health to make regulations for the review, on a regular basis, of children placed in residential care by the Health Boards. In particular, Health Boards will be required to consider whether it would be in the best interests of the child to be given into the custody of his or her parents.

Mental Health

292.   Under the Constitution a person may request that an inquiry be carried out by the High Court if he or she believes that his or her detention is unlawful. Under the Mental Treatment Act, 1945, any person may apply to the Minister for Health for an order for the examination by two medical practitioners of a detained patient and the Minister may, if he or she thinks fit, on consideration of their reports, direct the discharge of the patient. The Minister for Health may also arrange for an examination of the patient by the Inspector of Mental Hospitals and may direct his or her charge where justified.

293.   The new White Paper on Mental Health Legislation proposes that a Mental Health
        Review Board will be established by law which would have the necessary
        independence to carry out its functions in an impartial way. The function of the Board
        would be to review every decision to detain a mentally disordered person, including
        children, to hear appeals against orders detaining patients and to review the detention
        of long-stay patients.

VII. BASIC HEALTH AND WELFARE

A. Survival and Development (Art.6, para.2)

294.   Perinatal and infant mortality in Ireland are now at the lowest levels ever achieved, and the decline can be expected to continue, though at a less dramatic rate than in previous decades. Rates are now less than a third of what they were thirty years ago, and Ireland compares very favourably with other developed countries. For the most recent available year (1991), the perinatal mortality rate stood at 9.4 deaths per 1,000 live and still births. Ireland has a rate of 5.9 in the case of infant mortality, although the infant mortality rate for the Travelling Community is significantly above the national average (see paragraph 626).

295.   These reductions in mortality have been achieved through improvements in living conditions as well as in the standard and uptake of maternal care. Birth rates in Ireland have been falling quite rapidly since 1980, and the underlying fertility rates have been gradually declining over a much longer period. The number of birth annually has fallen from a high of 74,064 in 1980 to 47,929 registered births in 1994. Irish birth and fertility rates are now approaching those of other EU countries. This fact, together with advances in obstetric care and increasing promotion and awareness among mothers of the importance of antenatal care and healthy lifestyles, should ensure that the survival rates and health development of children continue to improve.

296.   In Ireland, as in other developed countries, the single greatest threat to the survival of children once they have passed the infant stage, at twelve months, comes from accidents. In 1994, 52 children between the ages of 1 and 14 were registered as having died due to accidents. This accounts for 33% of all deaths in this age group. Of these deaths, approximately half (25) were due to road traffic accidents.

297.   The maternity and infant care service, the national childhood immunisation programme, the public health nursing service and the pre-school and the school health service are significant elements in the provision of child health. These services are dealt with in greater detail under Article 24.

298.   Media campaigns are also undertaken to create a greater public awareness of the importance of immunisation.

299.   Ireland administers a scheme of Maternity Benefit and Maternity Leave for women in employment (either full-time or part-time). Such women are entitled to social security benefit up to a maximum of fourteen consecutive weeks at the time of childbirth, provided they satisfy the appropriate social insurance contribution conditions. It is a condition of the scheme that payment begins not later than four weeks prior to the expected date of birth.

300. Benefit is paid, per week, at the rate of 70% of average weekly earnings in the last complete tax year before the year in which the claim is made, subject to a minimum and maximum payment limit. An additional feature of the scheme allows a claimant the option, where favourable, to receive the rate corresponding to that of Disability Benefit, provided she satisfies the qualifying conditions for this scheme.

301. Women employed abroad as volunteer workers may also qualify for Maternity Allowance without having to satisfy the employment conditions attached to the scheme.

Maternity Leave

302. The Maternity Protection Act 1994 incorporates the employment rights aspect of the EU pregnant Workers Directive (92/85/EEC) into Irish Law. The Act covers any employee who is pregnant, who has recently given birth or who is breastfeeding and entitles such employees to 14 consecutive weeks' maternity leave, which attracts a social security payment in the majority of cases, and during which all employment rights, other than the right to remuneration, are guaranteed. It also entities them, at their own option, to additional, unpaid maternity leave of up to four weeks, which must follow on immediately from the maternity leave, during pregnancy and for the 14 week period following the birth, employees are entitled to time off work without loss of pay for ante-natal and post-natal medical visits.

303. The Act also provides that an employee shall be granted leave to protect her health and safety, whether because of risk to her in the workplace or arising from night work and where it is not feasible to provide suitable alternative work. For the first three weeks of health and safety leave employees are entitled to receive remuneration from their employers. For the remainder of such leave a social security benefit is payable to eligible employees. Following any absences authorised under the Act, an employee has the right to return to work in the same employment and under the same conditions that existed before the leave.

Adoptive Leave

304. The Adoptive Leave Act, 1995 provides an entitlement to a period of adoptive leave for female employees. Adoptive leave is also available to males where the man is a sole male adopter, and in other certain limited circumstances, namely where the adopting mother dies before the commencement of or during the leave.

305. The Act provides for a minimum period of 10 weeks adoptive leave, which attracts as social security payment in the majority of cases. An employee who has taken adoptive leave is entitled to avail of up to 4 weeks additional unpaid leave immediately following the period of adoptive leave. Following any absences authorised under the Act, an employee has the right to return to work in the same employment and under the same conditions that existed before the leave.

B.   Disabled Children (Art. 23)

306.   Overall policy is to assist children with a disability to live with their families. Where this is not possible, children are cared for in residential settings by Health Boards and voluntary organisations. The majority of children in residential care have severe or profound mental handicap or multiple handicaps. A large proportion of the services for persons with a disability, and in particular those with a mental handicap, are provided by voluntary organisations, both lay and religious. Traditionally it was the religious orders who became involved in the provision and development of services for persons with a mental handicap. Over the years however an increasing number of lay organisations, mainly parent and friend support groups, have become involved in the provision of services at community level. Funding for these organisations is provided, through the Health Boards, by the Department of Health. In addition, fourteen voluntary organisations providing services for people with mental handicap are funded directly by the Department of Health.

307.   Children with a disability who are accommodated in residential care are encouraged, as far as possible, to integrate into the social life of the local community. They are also helped to achieve their full potential in regard to social and educational skills.

308.   A range of support services are available to children with a disability. These include speech therapy, physiotherapy, occupational therapy, technical aids, audiology and residential care services. The National Rehabilitation Board (NRB), provides a number of direct services to people with disabilities including a technical aids information service, a national audiology service, psychological services, occupational guidance and training services. The NRB is organised on a regional basis and has offices in various parts of the country.

309.   Children with a mental handicap have access to development and assessment services and pre-school services. Developmental day care units care for children who, because of the degree or type of handicap, or their age, are unsuited to special schools. In recent years there has been considerable expansion of respite care and home support services to families caring for children with mental handicap at home.

310.   Considerable resources have also been invested in recent years in the provision of additional residential, day care and vocational training facilities. Despite this, however, there are still waiting lists for placement in such services, mainly as a result of the increased longevity of persons with a mental handicap. While most of those awaiting placement in services are adults, the waiting lists also include some children.

311.   At present the majority of children with a severe or profound mental handicap attend services provided through the health services rather than the educational services. The Department of Education is, however, extending its special educational programmes to include these children, who also continue to receive the necessary back up support from the health services.

312. A number of schemes exist which provide financial aid where a child is disabled. Many children with disabilities (e.g. mental handicap) are medical card holders which entitles them to free medical care (category 1 eligibility as described in paragraph 335) Under the income tax code, tax relief is extended to a person whose child (including stepchild, legally adopted child or informally adopted child) is permanently incapacitated.

Financial Assistance

313. Schemes to provide financial assistance in the case of a disabled child are administered by the Health Boards.

314. A Domiciliary Care Allowance is paid in respect of handicapped children between the ages of 2 and 16 years who require attention which is considerably in excess of that normally required by a child of the same age group. Eligibility is determined primarily by reference to the degree of care and attention required by the child rather than the handicap involved. The means of the parents are not taken into account when assessing eligibility but the child's means, e.g. compensation awards, are assessable.

315. A Disabled Person's Maintenance Allowance is a weekly allowance which is paid, subject to a medical and means test, to disabled persons over 16 years and under 66 years of age who are unable to work due to a disability. Responsibility for this scheme will be transferred from the Health Boards/Department of Health to the Department of Social Welfare in early 1996 on the basis that it is primarily an income support scheme.

316. A Long-Term Illness Scheme provides drugs and medicines free of charge to children with a disability for a number of specified illnesses including for example cystic fibrosis, spina bifida, hydrocephalous and multiple sclerosis.

317. Specialist child and adolescent psychiatric teams headed by consultant child and adolescent psychiatrists are in place in each of the eight Health Board regions. Arrangements are being made to further develop these specialist services in order to improve levels of care for children and adolescents with mental illness.

318. The Commission on the Status of People with Disabilities was established in November 1993. People with disabilities, their advocates and parents make up 60% of the membership. In essence, the Commission has been asked to find out how well the present system meets the needs and wishes of people with disabilities and to propose changes aimed at bringing about equality and full participation on their part. The Commission is examining a wide range of issues which impact on the daily lives of people with disabilities e.g. education, health, income support etc. In all its deliberations, the Commission assesses the needs of people with disabilities across all age groups and it is expected that its recommendations will benefit children.

319.   The Minister for Equality and Law Reform has indicated that he intends to establish a Council for the Status of People with Disabilities to oversee the implementation of Government policy in relation to people with disabilities, including children.

Education Policy

320.   During the past 30 years, a comprehensive system of special education has been provided for children with special needs, and in more recent times, special education services have been further expanded to cater for the needs of children with psychiatric, emotional and behavioural problems. At present some 0.9% of pupils of primary and second-level age receive their education in special schools.

321.   Government policy is to encourage the maximum possible level of participation and integration of children with special needs into ordinary schools, and to put in place the necessary special supports to facilitate this development and to ensure that the child has access to appropriate education, training, health-care and rehabilitation services, preparation for employment and recreational opportunities. Social integration and the fullest individual development of the child is the aim. In line with the recently-published White Paper on Education, Education Boards will have responsibility for coordinating educational provision, including support services, for students with special needs. A new scheme will also make provision for specialist computer-type equipment, at Primary and Post-Primary level, for pupils with cerebral palsy and similar disabilities.

322.   Where the condition of the child is more serious, placement in a special class attached to an ordinary school or placement in a special school may be the preferred option. A range of such special facilities, which enjoy preferential pupil-teacher ratios and funding, is provided. Each facility is equipped to cater for particular handicap groups.

323.   Teachers employed in special education services have the same initial training as teachers generally; this training includes modules directed at dealing with children with special needs. The initial training has traditionally been supplemented by various kinds of in-career development specifically suited to the needs of the client population.

324.   Implementation of the recommendations of the Special Education Review Committee (which was set up in 1991 to review existing services and make recommendations on the provision for children with special needs), has already commenced and an action plan, aimed at achieving the objectives set out in the report over the next four years, is in preparation. Additional teaching posts and child-care assistant posts are being made available in the special education area. Funding of special schools and classes has been substantially increased. Special financing has been allocated to facilitate the appointment of escorts to accompany seriously handicapped children on special school transport routes.

325.   Special arrangements are made in the certificate examinations for candidates who would have difficulty in communicating what they know to an examiner because of

a physical disability, including visual and hearing impairments, or a specific learning difficulty.

326. In 1994 there were 38 visiting teachers serving ordinary primary and second-level schools in certain areas of the country with children who have hearing and/or visual impairment or children with "Down's syndrome". Each visiting teacher serves a number of pupils in several schools.

327. A scheme for home tuition provides education in the home for pupils whose medical condition or disability prevents them from attending school or from attending school regularly. Recently, this scheme has been extended to cater for severely physically disabled pupils with severe speech problems who need additional help to operate computer equipment for the purpose of communication.

328. Teachers and educationalists from Ireland participate in seminars and study visits to European schools while their European counterparts visit Irish schools through the various programmes organised by the European Union, such as the Helios II programme, which aims at promoting the integration of pupils with disabilities into mainstream schools.

Transport Policy

329. The parents of a child with a disability may be entitled to tax concessions on the purchase or adapting of a motor vehicle for the transport of the child. The Government is also committed to improving access to public buildings and public transport for all people with disabilities.

330. The Department of Social Welfare also administers a Free Travel scheme, which while available to people resident in the State who are aged 66 or over, is also available to people under 66 years of age who are in receipt of a Disabled Person's Maintenance Allowance from their Health Board or an Invalidity pension from the Department of Social Welfare. Where a person cannot travel alone for medical reasons, they may be entitled to a Free Travel Companion Pass which allows a companion to accompany them free of charge. This pass is being extended, from July 1996, to blind and visually impaired children.

331. The national transport group, Coras Iompair Éireann (CIE) and its operating subsidiaries, Iarnród Éireann/Irish Rail, Bus Éireann and Dublin Bus are directly responsible for the provision of adequate and safe public transport services to all passengers, including the disabled. All new buses introduced to the fleets of Dublin Bus and Bus Éireann are designed to the recommended specifications issued by the Disabled Persons Transport Advisory Committee.

332. Dublin Bus, in association with the EU Horizon Initiative has introduced, on a pilot basis, an integrated bus service using low-floor wheelchair accessible vehicles on a fixed route in the capital city. This service will link the national railway company Iarnród

Éireann's suburban DART train service, to provide a through service to the city centre and beyond which will be fully accessible to wheelchair persons.

333.	It is Iarnród Éireann's policy to adapt its rolling stock and buildings to the needs of the mobility handicapped, in line with international guidelines and as resources permit.

## C.	Health and Health Services (Art. 24)

334.	All Irish residents are eligible to avail of a comprehensive and high-quality health service. There are two categories of eligibility. Persons in Category 1 include about 35% of the population and there is a means test for inclusion in this Category. The income guidelines include an allowance for each child in a family. In addition, persons whose income exceeds the guidelines may be given Category 1 eligibility if the Health Board considers that they are unable to provide general practitioner, medical and surgical services for themselves and their dependants. The Health Board can also give Category 1 eligibility to an individual child, where the family does not qualify, if the child has medical circumstances which justify it.

335.	People in Category 1 are entitled to services which include the following:

- general practitioner services;
- prescribed drugs and medicines;
- all in-patient public hospital services in public wards (including consultant services);
- all out-patient public hospital services (including consultant services);
- dental, ophthalmic and aural services and appliances;
- a maternity and infant care service. This includes the services of a family doctor during pregnancy and family doctor services for mother and baby for up to 6 weeks after the birth.

336.	People above the income guidelines for Category 1 are included in Category 2. Services in Category 2 include the following:

- all in-patient public hospital services in public wards, (including consultant services) subject to certain charges;

- out-patient public hospital services (including consultant services) subject to certain charges but excluding dental and routine ophthalmic and aural services. However, the latter exclusion does not apply in the case of referrals from a child health clinic or school health examination;

- all in-patient and out patient public hospital services in the case of referrals from a child health clinic or school health examination;

- a refund of expenditure on prescribed drugs and medicines over a certain sum per quarter or a refund of all expenditure over a certain fixed sum for people who, suffer from certain long-term medical conditions;

- drugs and medicines free for the treatment of certain specified illnesses under the Long-Term Illness Scheme.

337. In 1994 the Health Insurance Act came into effect. It introduced a new regulatory framework for health insurance in Ireland and is designed to allow for competition in the health insurance market. The regulations allow an infant born to a person named in a health insurance contract to be covered in the insurance contract from birth, providing that the parent names it in the contract and pays the appropriate premium within 13 weeks of the birth of the infant. The act allows for premiums for persons under the age of 18 years to be either waived or reduced by not more than 50%. It also allows the premium payable for a person aged 18 years and under 21 years in full time education and dependent on the person who has taken out the contract to be reduced by not more than 50%.

Voluntary Sector

338. The voluntary sector plays a role in the provision of health and personal social services in Ireland which is probably unique internationally. Traditionally, voluntary organisations have been to the forefront in identifying needs in the community and developing responses to them. Their independence enables them to harness community support and to complement the statutory services in an innovative and flexible way. Agencies in the voluntary sector range from major hospitals and national organisations to small community-based support groups set up in response to local needs. Some receive the bulk of their funding from the State, whether directly from the Department of Health or through the Health Boards; others receive some financial support to supplement the voluntary funds which they raise.

Child Health Service

339. The Child Health Service consists of a number of distinct components including the Maternity and Infant Care Service, the national primary childhood immunisation programme, the public health nursing service, the pre-school and the school health services. These services are designed to promote health in infants and children, to prevent illness and disease and to monitor the progress and development of infants and children with the aim of identifying and rectifying defects at an early stage.

Maternity and Infant Care Service

340. Maternity services are provided by dedicated maternity hospitals and also by maternity units within some general hospitals. The overwhelming majority of the 49,500 births per annum take place in these hospitals, staffed by consultant obstetricians,

paediatricians and midwives. There are approximately 1,000 obstetric beds and over 366 gynaecology beds throughout the country.

341.   An ante-natal and post-natal service (including out-patient care) is available without charge to all women from general practitioners and public maternity hospitals. The service provided has been and continues to be of a high standard with regard to protecting the lives and health of mothers and new born infants. The quality of services available in the larger maternity hospitals has attracted women from other countries and the education and training courses on offer have acquired an international reputation for excellence.

342.   A review of the Maternity and Infant care scheme has been completed and the report is currently under consideration.

National Childhood Immunisation Programme

343.   Under the national primary childhood immunisation programme, immunisation against a number of infectious diseases is provided free of charge. The programme is promoted and delivered by the State on a voluntary basis.

344.   The current national rate of vaccination of young children, as reported to the Department of Health by the Health Boards, ranges from approximately 90% availing of protection against Diphtheria, Tetanus and Polio to 60% having received the vaccine against Pertussis. The estimated current uptake of the Measles, Mumps and Rubella (MMR) vaccination at 15 months is approximately 75%. However, a very high uptake level (over 90%), is being achieved in the school-based booster MMR immunisation programme introduced in 1992 for 10-14 year-old children .

345.   There are a number of deficiencies in the current primary childhood immunisation system, which are being addressed as part of the implementation of the Health Strategy "Shaping a Healthier Future". One of these deficiencies is the absence of computerisation in some areas and an inadequate system of reporting by general practitioners on vaccinations carried out so that it is not possible to assess uptake levels accurately.

346.   During the first half of 1995 a measles immunisation campaign was conducted by Health Boards. The campaign was aimed at unimmunised primary school children and was delivered by the Health Board's community care medical staff. It will ensure a very high level of protection against measles and rubella among primary school children.

347.   A review of the National Childhood Immunisation Programme has been completed and the reorganisation of the programme, with the objective of achieving a 95% uptake, is being negotiated. Henceforth, the National Primary Childhood Immunisation Programme will be delivered by general practitioners and will be free of charge to all children.

Public Health Nursing Service

348. All new babies are visited and examined by the Public Health Nurse within a short period after discharge from the maternity hospital/unit. Babies continue to be seen regularly by the Public Health Nurse up to 3 years of age. Where a family has additional needs the Public Health Nurse visits as required and up to the age of 6 years if necessary.

Paediatric hospital services

349. There are three specialist paediatric hospitals in Dublin, the National Children's Hospital, Harcourt Street, Our Lady's Hospital for Sick Children, Crumlin and Temple Street Hospital with a total complement of 470 beds. Twenty-five acute general hospitals throughout the country have a total of 745 specialist paediatric beds.

350. Our Lady's Hospital for Sick Children, Crumlin is the national centre for paediatric surgery, bone marrow and liver transplant services for children. Crumlin Hospital also provides an oncology service for children throughout the country. The National Metabolic Screening Laboratory is located in Temple Street Hospital, Dublin.

351. There were 1,449 children on hospital waiting lists as at December, 1994. These figures included those waiting for the problem specialities of Ear, Nose and Throat surgery, Ophthalmology, Cardiac Surgery, and General Surgery. The proportion of children waiting over six months of treatment fell from almost 56% at the end of March, 1994 to 40% at the end of December 1994.

352. In addition, within the overall figures there has been a number of significant advances. For instance, during 1994 the plastic surgery waiting list for children which includes those waiting for treatment for conditions such as cleft palate, fell from 462 to 190, a reduction of 58%. The number of children waiting over six months for ear nose and throat procedures such as tonsil and adenoid operations and for grommets fell by 60% from 691 to 277.

Pre-School Examination

353. The pre-school health service is based on a comprehensive developmental paediatric examination which is available for all children at the approximate ages of 6-9 months, 12-15 months and 24 months. These examinations take place at a local health centre.

School Health Service

354. The School Health Service is based on a comprehensive medical examination of children in designated classes and/or a system of selective examinations (where children are brought to the attention of the medical officer by the parent or teacher). Normally these examinations are carried out in the school by Health Board

community care medical staff. All necessary follow-up services for problems discovered during these examinations are provided free of charge.

Dental Services

355.   Community Dental Services are currently provided free to children until their fourteenth birthday, by State employed dentists. It is proposed to extend eligibility for dental services to children up to the age of 16 years.

356.   Because of the high cost of fixed appliance orthodontic therapy, the Health Boards can only provide this treatment where a child has a severe handicapping orthodontic condition. Children are assessed, therefore, in accordance with guidelines drawn up by the Department of Health to ensure that resources are used to best advantage and for those most in need of treatment.

357.   The National Health Strategy "Shaping a Healthier Future," which will be implemented over the next four years aims to achieve many oral health goals by the year 2000.

Ophthalmic Services

358.   Ophthalmic Services are provided free of charge to children who attend primary school. Health Boards provide (normally through the school health examination system) sight-testing services, examine eye defects, and, where necessary, prescribe spectacles or refer children to specialists for treatment. Spectacles are provided by private opticians to children where required following examination.

Aural Services

359.   Aural Services are provided free to children who attend primary school. Children are screened for hearing defects at pre-school and school health examinations, usually by public health nurses with specialised training and where necessary referred for further treatment. The National Rehabilitation Board's Audiology Service provides audiometry tests for children referred by health authorities and supplies and repairs hearing aids for children.

Health Promotion

360.   Steps have been taken by the Health Promotion Unit of the Department of Health to diminish infant and child mortality and morbidity through media campaigns highlighting the advantages of immunisation, and dissemination of a wide range of materials and publications through maternity hospitals, health centres and GP clinics.

361.   Information is available from the Health Promotion Unit to women before they become pregnant on how they should prepare for pregnancy e.g. consuming adequate

amounts of folic acid in order to prevent neural tube defects. A range of other literature provides advice on preparing for childbirth and post-natal care.

362. A report on a National Breast-Feeding Policy for Ireland was prepared for the Department of Health and launched in July 1994. This policy sets specific targets which aim to increase the rate of breast feeding in Ireland. The report was widely disseminated to relevant organisations, which were requested to reply to the Health Promotion Unit of the Department of Health outlining the steps being taken to implement the recommendations in the report.

363. Information is also disseminated on a countrywide basis regarding the prevention of accidents and on reducing the risk of cot death.

364. A Nutrition Framework for Action published in 1991 addressed the issues of adult and child nutrition. As a result of this Framework a number of measures have been put in place to inform and educate the general population, specifically parents and their children, about healthy eating.

365. A Health Promotion Strategy was launched by the Minister for Health in July, 1995 and presents a detailed strategy for the promotion of health in Ireland. The document provides a review of the current health status of the Irish population and sets out a detailed programme containing specific goals and targets for their achievement. Children form one of the priority population groups focused on in the strategy.

Teenage Pregnancy

366. In the Health Promotion Strategy, the Health Promotion Unit of the Department of Health identified the need for the development of appropriate programmes to reduce teenage pregnancies and to respond to the needs of teenagers who become pregnant.

367. The Unit has therefore provided a grant to the Eastern Health Board for the development of a pilot programme to reduce teenage pregnancies. The programme aims not only to reduce teenage pregnancies but to provide information and also to alter attitudes and behaviour of young people in relation to sexual activity. In doing this, emphasis is placed on decision making, taking responsibility, communication skills and self esteem enhancement. The programme is small in scale but the report on the programme is being considered by the Inter- Departmental Committee of the Departments of Health and Education on Relationships and Sex Education and the findings will be useful in determining future direction in this area. In addition a group of Eastern Health Board personnel are examining the outcome of the programme with a view to its wider dissemination.

Births inside and outside Marriage to Mothers aged 18 years or under and as a percentage of births to mothers of all ages, 1991 to 1994. *				
	Births inside Marriage	Births outside Marriage	Total Number	As a % of All Births
1991	117	1483	1600	3.0
1992	97	1410	1507	2.9
1993	93	1391	1484	3.0
1994	62	1308	1370	2.9

* Provisional figures as they relate to births registered and not to births occurring during those years.

Health Education

368. In Ireland, health education in schools developed initially in relation to specific issues/problems such as abuse of legal and illegal drugs, AIDS and cancer prevention. As it became clear that preventive education should be concerned with life-styles and issues concerned with overall development of the person, health education has evolved into an aspect of the general social and personal development education provided in schools.

369. A curriculum development committee is currently considering all aspects of health education provision. Co-operation between education and health agencies and voluntary bodies, at central and local level is a feature of the developing approach. Co-operation with parents is regarded as essential.

370. The main projects developed or in hand are as follows:

- A number of co-operative projects on health education are in place between schools and Health Boards. These have developed programmes and provided training for teachers;

- A project entitled the Health-Promoting School is underway in a number of primary and second-level schools. The basic aim is to develop a whole-school approach to health promotion with links to parents and the community and an emphasis on social and personal development;

- A HIV/AIDS Educational Resource Package for second-level schools was developed by the Departments of Education and Health. After a very successful pilot phase these materials were distributed to each second-level school in the country in 1990 and all schools were offered an in-service training day. The materials aim to provide information for pupils on the causes, transmission and prevention of AIDS, to help them explore attitudes to AIDS and to promote a mature attitude among pupils in assuming responsibility for their own health and the health of others.

- A package of Substance Abuse Prevention Education materials has been completed and is being disseminated to second-level schools;

- The Department of Education co-operated with the Department of Health and the Irish Cancer Society in the school based activities of the Europe Against Cancer Programme 1990-94. Further co-operation in the next five-year programme is planned;

- A Child Abuse Prevention Programme - "Stay Safe" - devised by the Eastern Health Board with the support of the Health Promotion Unit and designed to prevent the problems of bullying and child abuse is available to all primary schools throughout the country. A team of social workers and teachers has provided in-service training for primary teachers from all schools. The implementation of the programme involves parental as well as children's education;

- The Minister for Education has asked that schools begin to put in place a Programme of Relationships and Sexuality Education during the school year 1995/96. The development of this programme is being overseen by a group representative of the Partners in Education and by an inter-departmental group consisting of the Departments of Health and Education;

- A guide to hygiene and infection control in schools has been published by the Department of Health.

- A nutrition education programme for primary schools has been developed by the Department of Health and by the Department of Education and by the North Western Health Board. This programme has been successfully piloted and will be widely available from 1996 onwards.

- A smoking cessation and reduction action programme for second level schools has been developed by the Departments of Health and Education with the Irish Cancer Society. This programme has been piloted, evaluated and will be available during the 1995/96 school year.

Alcohol Abuse

371. Alcohol abuse in Ireland is a matter that can have negative consequences for the enjoyment by children of the rights protected and promoted under the Convention. Alcohol is a drug which can lead to significant problems both for the individual, and for the community at large, when taken to excess on any occasion or consistently taken in large amounts for a long period of time. These problems impact on the health

of the nation and have implications for road safety, the workplace, violence, and crime & poverty levels in society.

372. The report on the development of the psychiatric services, **PLANNING FOR THE FUTURE**, published in 1984, referred to the trend in Ireland towards greater specialisation in the management of alcohol related problems. The approach often involved costly in-patient care which tended to separate the treatment and management of alcohol related problems from community medical and social services.

373. The Report questioned the wisdom of this approach on the following grounds:

(a) There was no evidence that intensive, high cost in-patient treatment was in any way superior to simple, inexpensive community-based intervention. Compared with the later form of management, the intensive approach was not considered to be cost effective.

(b) The overspecialised approach to alcohol related problems was also a separatist approach. It drew the problem away from the community and family, and tended to exclude the contribution of primary care and community medical and social services from the management of the problem. To that extent, it ran contrary to the general principles of the delivery of health care which stresses that help to individuals and families should be as near to their communities and homes as possible.

374. In accordance with World Health Organisation opinion, the Report recommended that in future the emphasis should be on the prevention of alcohol related problems, the Report acknowledged that there were no preventive measures immediately in sight and that treatment would continue to be necessary. The Report recommended that, as far as possible, these problems should be dealt with at a community level by primary health care and social services. One reason for this is that the problems occur in local and family settings and therefore the community-based response will be earlier.

375. Arising out of the White Paper on new mental health legislation recently published, the new legislation in this area will ensure that addiction to alcohol will no longer be grounds for involuntary detention in a psychiatric in-patient facility as it is at present under the Mental Treatment Act, 1945 and subsequent amending legislation.

376. It is now considered that the emphasis in relation to alcohol related problems should be on their prevention. This is a key element in the promotion of moderation in the consumption of alcohol to reduce the risks to physical, mental and family health which arise from alcohol misuse. The National Health Strategy, **SHAPING A HEALTHIER FUTURE**, made a commitment to the publication of a National Alcohol Policy which will address the broader economic, cultural and health factors which impinge on alcohol use and misuse and will be published in the near future.

Incidence of Alcohol Abuse

377. Consumption of pure alcohol per head of population peaked in 1979 and has shown a slight decrease since then. One area of particular concern in recent years is the evidence that drinking levels among young people has increased.

378. A 1991 survey of alcohol use among a national sample of second year post primary school students found the average age for a first drinking episode was 12.6 years. The survey found that 38.5% of all those surveyed had consumed at least one whole alcoholic drink in their lifetime, 30.2% were found to be current drinkers (19.6% moderate category; 10.6% abuse category). Over a third (34.4%) of all males surveyed and over a quarter of all females surveyed were found to be current drinkers (ie. drinking with varying degrees of frequency ranging from, at the very least, once or twice a year to as often as every weekend). 35.2% of those classified as current drinkers were abusing alcohol.

379. In 1994, 50 persons in the 15-19 age group were admitted to psychiatric hospitals due to alcoholic disorders and there was one admission of an individual under the age of 15 years. Data is not available in respect of the number of individuals who may have received treatment in a community-based setting.

380. In order to examine current drinking behaviour of respondents, three categories, based on response scores were established, namely; (i) abstainer or virtual abstainer (ii) moderate and (iii) abuse. The abstainer or virtual abstainer category refers to non-drinkers. Current drinkers are divided between the moderate and abuse categories. The distinction between these latter two categories is one of degree rather than kind. Inclusion in the abuse category is usually characterised by a significant and more frequent alcohol intake together with the endorsement of such items as drinking to get drunk, drinking to intoxication, drinking alone and experiencing physical and/or behavioural consequences of alcohol abuse.

Prevention Programmes

381. The Health Promotion Unit has a number of substance prevention initiatives in place. The programmes which have been developed not only highlight the dangers of substance misuse but also give people the opportunity to develop the skills necessary to resist pressures to use various substances of abuse.

382. These include a comprehensive programme for second level schools developed in association with the Department of Education and the Mater Dei Counselling Centre. The programme entitled "On My Own Two Feet" has now been introduced to about 50 per cent of second level schools. It is a participatory programme concentrating on identity and self-esteem; assertive communication; feelings; influences on young people; and decision making.

383.   A Drink Awareness for Youth programme is also available through the National Youth Council of Ireland. It is a joint initiative between the Health Promotion Unit, the National Youth Council of Ireland and the Department of Education. The principal aim of the programme is to increase awareness within society generally, and among young people especially, of the effects, consequences and dangers involved in the misuse or abuse of alcohol.

384.   Programmes for use in community settings have also developed. In addition the Health Promotion Unit develop and distribute a series of booklets, leaflets and posters on the subject of alcohol.

Health and Smoking Policy

385.   While the numbers of smokers has fallen from 43% of the adult population in the 1970s to 28% currently, smoking remains a major cause of illness and premature death. Current levels of illness and premature death in Ireland are largely due to cancer and cardiovascular disease. Smoking is regarded as the main cause of cancer and one of the main causes of cardiovascular disease. There is also an increasing demand from non-smokers to be protected from the harmful effects of passive smoking and to enjoy a smoke-free environment.

386.   An Action Plan to further reduce the incidence of smoking in Ireland was announced on 31 May 1995 to coincide with World No-Smoking Day. This plan is intended to support the achievement of the target set in the National Health Strategy, to reduce the proportion of those who smoke to 20% of the population by the year 2000.

Smoking in Public Places

387.   The Tobacco Health Promotion and Protection Regulations, 1990, prohibit smoking in public areas in state and semi-state buildings, schools, most areas of universities, all food preparation areas, supermarkets and grocery stores, bus and railway stations, indoor sports centres, cinemas, theatres, concert halls, art galleries and museums, buses and the DART system. In addition, smoking in health premises, restaurants, trains, aircraft, and seating areas in airports and harbours, is restricted to specified areas.

388.   It has been announced that the existing controls will be strengthened and extended in response to the marked increase in public concern about the effects of passive smoking. It is intended to extend the ban on smoking to a number of new areas including creches and playschools; doctors and dentists waiting rooms; retail pharmacies; Bingo halls and bowling alleys; public areas in banks, building societies and other financial institutions, and in hairdressing salons, barber shops and taxis.

389.   In addition, it is intended to ban smoking in health facilities, such as hospitals, residential centres etc. where smoking is at present banned in designated "no-smoking" areas. The only exception will be that specific facilities may be provided for staff and patients to smoke.

390. The proportion of the seating in restaurants, airports, harbours, trains and aircraft which is designated as "no-smoking" will be reviewed and extended to passenger ferries. This will be done following consultation with the various representative groups. The national airline, Aer Lingus, already operates a no-smoking policy on all flights in response to customer preference.

Prisons

391. Doctors are assigned on a part time basis to each prison and place of detention, with the exception of open centres where local doctors attend as necessary. Doctors are responsible, in general, for the medical welfare of offenders and are obliged to provide care to a standard at least equivalent to that in the wider community. They are also required to pay particular attention to offenders with psychiatric problems and doctors also regularly inspect food, sanitation, kitchens, bedding, ventilation etc. In the case of pregnant prisoners, appropriate pre-natal and post-natal care is provided to the same standards as apply in the community. In practice such women attend local maternity hospitals on a regular basis and arrangements are in place for their children to be born in a hospital outside the prison.

392. Visiting psychiatrists are available to provide on-going psychiatric care and there are arrangements in place for in-patient psychiatric treatment in the Central Mental Hospital.

Transport Policy

393. The national bus company Bus Éireann, as the administrators and operators of the School Transport Scheme on behalf of the Department of Education, takes all possible steps to ensure that the 165,000 children catered for under the scheme are conveyed in a safe manner. There are ongoing safety campaigns to make teachers, parents and children aware of the hazards encountered while travelling to and from school.

394. The national train company Iarnród Éireann produces posters and leaflets which are distributed to schools and displayed at stations. They are aimed at accident prevention and the reduction of vandalism.

395. The initiatives reported under Article 23 in respect of improved facilities for the mobility handicapped have also served to improve the safety and user-friendliness of buses and trains for children and mothers with babies.

396. Reduced fares for children are offered by public transport companies, including special schoolchild half-fare rates.

Health, Control Standards and Foodstuffs

397. Implementation of health and control standards in relation to primary production and processing stages in the manufacture of foodstuffs is given high priority. These

standards and control procedures ensure that in so far as this part of the food chain is concerned, foodstuffs reach a high acceptable standard for all consumers, in particular the three most vulnerable groups, viz. children, the ill and the elderly.

398.   Maximum Residue Limits (MRLs) have been established to protect the health of consumers and to facilitate trade. The MRLs established for individual commodities are such that the acceptable daily intake (ADI) levels for individual pesticides are not exceeded. The effects of exposure over the entire lifetime, as well as exposures of a shorter duration, are taken into account in establishing ADI values. In all cases, the ADI values established include a safety factor to take account of the vulnerability of particular groups such as infants and children.

399.   Commodities consumed by infants and children and those used to manufacture prepared foods for infants and children are routinely sampled and analysed for their pesticide residue content. The results of the monitoring and enforcement programme are published annually.

400.   When ADI values relating to residues of veterinary drugs in food of animal origin e.g., antibiotics, chemotherapeutics, etc. are being established, account is taken of the special sensitivities of children.

401.   An ongoing monitoring programme is carried out in conjunction with the Radiological Protection Institute of Ireland to ensure that radioactivity levels in agricultural products comply with the requirements of EU Regulations and are safe for human consumption. In the case of milk products, Ireland observes the stringent levels set by the EU in order to protect children.

402.   All farm structures grant aided from both National and EU funds must comply with detailed specifications and standards on design, construction and safety laid down by the Department of Agriculture, Food and Forestry. These specifications and standards are based on relevant EU and National Standards for safety, welfare, hygiene, materials etc. and best practices for the industry and are subject to ongoing review. Over recent years, standards have been updated to reflect the latest requirements in the area of farm safety and particularly making farm structures as child-safe as possible.

Road Safety

403.   The National Safety Council, established in 1987, has a general brief to promote road safety through promotional campaigns, education and publicity, and plays the key role in national road safety campaigns.

404.   The main thrust of road safety strategy has been directed at changing public attitudes to road safety issues by way of extensive and sustained advertising and educational campaigns which highlight specific road safety issues. As part of the ongoing national campaign there are advertising campaigns highlighting safe child road-user behaviour e.g. the benefits of wearing cycle helmets, adequate lights on bicycles and wearing of

reflective armbands. At the commencement of the school year a "Back to School" campaign is undertaken using television and radio advertising, outdoor posters and leaflets targeting both parents and school children.

405.   Child road safety is specifically addressed through an extensive education programme which targets school children of both primary and post primary age. National Safety Council road safety officers make regular calls to schools delivering lectures and showing videos highlighting road safety awareness.

Seat Belts

406.   Most cars in Ireland are now fitted with front seat belts and there is now a legal requirement to have rear seat belts in newly registered cars. Where they are fitted it is compulsory for both adults and children to wear them. However, some older cars registered before 1971 may not have seat belts and where this is the case it is not obligatory for the owner of the car to have them fitted.

Air Quality

407.   National air quality standards, reflecting similar EU standards, are in force for smoke, sulphur dioxide, nitrogen oxide and lead. A review of air quality in Ireland over the ten year period 1981-1991 confirmed that acidification and industrial/transport related forms of air pollution do not pose significant problems. Ireland's air quality is generally good and a range of measures is being pursued to maintain this quality and to meet national and international emission standards.

Water Quality

408.   Ireland is favourably situated as regards water resources and a substantial legislative framework is in place to control water pollution.

409.   The bulk of surface waters are of high quality (almost 80% are unpolluted) and are capable of supporting the most sensitive uses, including water supply and game fishing. Ground-water reserves constitute a major natural resource and, although they are vulnerable to pollution, overall quality is good and there is no evidence of significant or widespread contamination.

D.   Social Security and Child Care Services and Facilities (Art. 26 and Art. 18, para. 3) and Standard of Living (Art. 27, paras. 1-3)

410.   A range of measures exist within the Irish social welfare code to provide financial support and assistance to families with children. These range from direct income-maintenance provisions to educational and employment initiatives. Such payments are

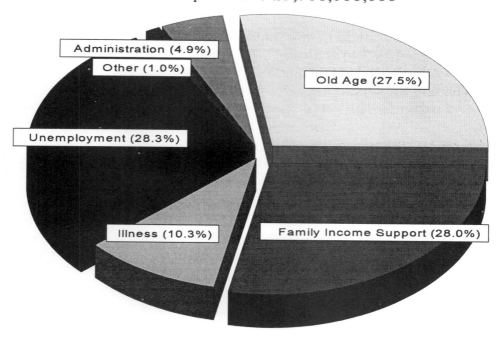

Expenditure on Social Welfare by Programme, 1994
Total Expenditure £3,761,066,000

- Administration (4.9%)
- Other (1.0%)
- Old Age (27.5%)
- Unemployment (28.3%)
- Illness (10.3%)
- Family Income Support (28.0%)

non-discriminatory, generally not gender-specific and adhere to the principle of equality between men and women.

411. The family unit, including single-parent families, is central to all Irish social welfare schemes. Due to the changing nature of families in present-day society, the social welfare process in Ireland is constantly reassessed and adapted to support the family. In the past, the main function of social welfare schemes was to provide income maintenance; today this role has been expanded, with a view to providing self-help and support measures designed to enhance the integrity and capability of the family to meet its own needs.

412. Total social security expenditure in 1994 was £3,761 million, which represented 33.6% of current Government expenditure and was equivalent to 12.1% of Gross National Product. The main areas of expenditure by programme were Unemployment, Old Age, Family Income Support and Illness. Administration of the social welfare system accounted for 4.9% of total expenditure.

413. It has been acknowledged by successive Irish governments that there may be weaknesses in the interaction between the system of personal taxation and the social welfare system. Criticism has been levelled at the complexity of, and lack of cohesion between the two systems in the treatment of income and the negative effect on the incentive to work, stemming from the interaction over certain income ranges, between loss of means-tested entitlements and the impact of progressive income tax. An Expert Group on the Integration of the Tax and Social Welfare systems was set up in June 1993 and it is expected that its final report will be available shortly. The Government is committed to taking action to remedy defects in this area.

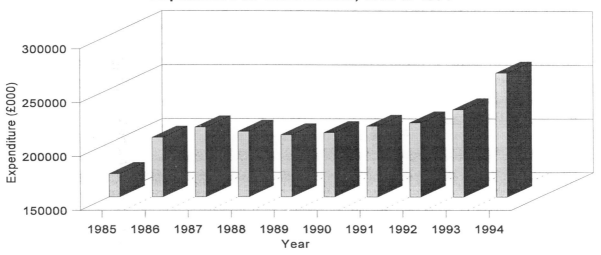

Expenditure on Child Benefit, 1985 to 1994

414. Reforms of the tax and social insurance systems in recent years have concentrated on creating a better climate for employment by offering incentives in the employer social insurance contribution for the employment of long-term unemployed and by easing costs on the employment of workers in the lower income range; and on the personal taxation side, by improving the take-home pay of lower paid workers in order to strengthen the incentive to seek and stay in work. Recent reforms on the benefits side, aimed at bolstering the in-work income of families with children through a major increase in universal child benefit, have had the same aim.

Taxation and Low Income Families

415. In order to reduce the tax burden of low income families, a Marginal Relief System is in operation. Under this system, incomes below certain limits are exempt from taxation, while incomes slightly above the limits are taxed at a special rate until such time as it would be more beneficial for the taxpayer to be taxed under the normal tax system.

416. Persons who are taxed under the marginal relief system are treated more favourably than taxpayers generally. The exemption limits which form the basis of their tax free allowances are considerably higher than the normal personal allowances. Marginal relief is made even more beneficial by additional allowances in respect of dependent children which are not available under the normal tax system. As a result, taxpayers on marginal relief pay less than they would under the normal system of taxation.

Child Benefit

417. The payment of Child Benefit is covered by sections 192-196 of the Social Welfare (Consolidation) Act, 1993. This payment is at the core of the Social Welfare Code, and is universal, non-contributory, and is not subject to an assessment of the parents means. Child Benefit is payable at a flat rate for the first two children and a higher rate for each subsequent child. Payment is normally paid to the mother or the primary

carer. Since 1995, a 45% increase in Child Benefit has been provided in respect of the first two children and a 36% increase for other children.

418.   Child Benefit is paid up to age 16 years, or age 18 if the child is in full-time education, physically or mentally handicapped or engaged in courses run by FÁS (the State's employment training authority) where an allowance is not payable.

419.   A special grant of IR£500 per child is paid on the birth of twins and at ages 4 and 12 to assist with the particular points of financial pressure as the children enter primary and post-primary schools. In the case of the birth of triplets or more, a special grant of IR£100 per child is paid, subject to a maximum payment of IR£400 for four or more children, Child Benefit is paid at double the normal monthly rate for each child so long as at least three of the children remain qualified.

420.   The Government has also signalled its intention to provide a new type of child income support, through the creation of a Child Benefit Supplement. This supplement will be payable in addition to the universal Child Benefit, to all families whose income is below a certain level - irrespective of whether that income is from social welfare or employment, or a combination of the two. It is intended that this will incorporate both the Child Dependent Allowances which are paid to people on social welfare and the Family Income Supplement payable to people in low paid employment.

Number of Families Receiving Child Benefit and Number of Child Beneficiaries, 1985 to 1994		
Year	Families	Children
1985	474971	1187465
1986	476149	1177087
1987	475844	1163347
1988	473697	1143183
1989	471837	1122702
1990	473232	1108561
1991	476411	1097447
1992	476086	1078690
1993	482300	1074735
1994	482592	1055156

Family Income Supplement

421.	The Family Income Supplement Scheme (F.I.S.) is a weekly cash allowance paid to families on low pay. It is intended to ensure that there is an incentive for people with families to take up and stay in work. Various exemptions in the income tax code are designed to the same end.

Expenditure on Family Income Supplement, 1985 to 1994	
Year	Expenditure (£000)
1985	2211
1986	3020
1987	4373
1988	5022
1989	6323
1990	8745
1991	10370
1992	12631
1993	16438
1994	20825

Orphan's Allowance

422.	The granting of an Orphan's Allowance is governed by sections 106-109 of the Social Welfare (Consolidation) Act, 1993. It is paid in respect of an orphaned child, resident in the State, under age 18 (or 21 if in full-time education) and who is dependent on a guardian.

Supplementary Welfare Allowance

423.	The payment of Supplementary Welfare Allowance is governed by sections 170-191 of the Social Welfare (Consolidation) Act, 1993. This is intended to be a speedy source of minimum safety-net income to individuals and families in need. Supplementary income maintenance is also provided for under this programme in addition to provision under other Social Welfare schemes.

Back to School Allowance

424.   The Back to School Clothing and Footwear Allowance is designed to help towards the cost of children's school uniforms and footwear at the beginning of the school year. It operates from 1 June to 30 September and benefits some 114,000 families with 270,000 children.

School Meals Scheme

425.   A "School Meals" scheme is administered by certain local councils with the aim of providing meals for children attending primary level schools. Fifty per cent of the cost of the food supplied is refunded to the councils by the Department of Social Welfare.

Lone Parent's Allowance

426.   Lone Parent's Allowance is covered by sections 157-162 of the Social Welfare (Consolidation) Act, 1993. The scheme is available to lone parents who are bringing up a child or children without the support of a partner. This scheme incorporates payments for those who are widowed, unmarried, separated/deserted or the spouse/partner of a prisoner, where the person has the care of at least one dependent child.

427.   Aware of the difficulties encountered by some people with the requirement to prove desertion in order to qualify for social welfare benefit or allowance in situations of marriage breakdown, the Government has proposed integrating the existing Lone Parent's Allowance and Deserted Wife's benefit into a uniform scheme for parents, men or women, caring for children on their own and abolishing the requirement to prove desertion. Details of this scheme are being finalised.

Homemakers/Care of Children

428.   In a further move to facilitate those parents who wish to care for their child or children for a period of time, Irish social security legislation provides special arrangements to facilitate entitlement to the Old Age Contributory Pension. Since April 1994, contribution years spent out of the workforce caring either for children aged up to 12 years or incapacitated people, will be disregarded when entitlement to pension is calculated.

Voluntary and Community Sector

429.   Ireland fully recognises that tackling economic and social problems requires a partnership approach. Partnerships between the State, the Social Partners and voluntary and community sectors have been forged allowing for participation in processes which affect decision-making. An example of such an initiative is the National Economic and Social Forum which represents a broad range of interests. In consultation with the voluntary and state sectors, a White Paper on Voluntary

Activity is under preparation which will set out a clear framework for partnership between the State and the voluntary sector and develop a cohesive strategy for supporting voluntary activity.

430.   A key objective of the Local Development Programme, which is designed to bring about social and economic development at local level, is to enable local communities to be centrally involved in that development. ADM Limited, which implements the Programme, supports community organisations so that they are enabled to participate fully in the partnership process, with the Social Partners and the State Agencies, at local level.

431.   The Department of Social Welfare plays a role in supporting local self-help and community development initiatives, complementing its more traditional role as administrator of income support schemes. It seeks to help people develop the confidence and the capacity to participate as partners alongside statutory agencies and others in local development initiatives. This support has been made available through a range of grant schemes.

432.   These grant schemes concentrate on support for local self-help groups, Community Development, welfare rights and information work, and on the provision of seed money to enable community groups to pilot initiatives identified as meeting new and emerging community needs. In 1994, funding of IR£6.73 million was provided, increasing to IR£ 7.96 million in 1995. The allocation for 1996 will be in excess of IR£ 9 million. The range of activities undertaken include home management programmes, counselling and advice services, self development programmes, community education, health programmes, parenting skills, literacy programmes, anti-moneylending and financial advice and self-help, leadership skills and community development.

433.   The Combat Poverty Agency is a state sponsored body established under the Combat Poverty Agency Act, 1986. The Board of Directors is appointed by the Minister for Social Welfare. The role off the agency is to advise the Government on economic and social policy in relation to poverty, evaluate measures aimed at overcoming poverty, examine the nature, causes and extent of poverty along with the promotion, commissioning and interpretation of research and the promotion of greater public understanding of the cause and effect of poverty.

434.   As acknowledged in paragraph 40 unemployment can have a damaging effect on the enjoyment of the rights of children under the Convention. Several initiatives have been put in to place aimed at reducing unemployment

Local Development programme

435.   The Operational Programme for Local Urban and Rural Development covers the period 1994-1999. The primary objective of the Programme is to provide a framework in which communities and individuals will become the prime movers in an integrated approach which will promote enterprise creation and employment, integrate the long

term unemployed and other marginalised groups into the labour market, promote education and training measures to tackle exclusion and marginalisation resulting from long term unemployment, early school leaving and poverty and regenerate the environment in cities, towns and villages.

436.   Measures which provide additional supports to facilitate participation in and benefit from education including at primary level, for those at risk of early school leaving and under-achievement leading to exclusion, can be funded under the Programme.

437.   Assistance is also provided to Organisations with a capacity to make a significant contribution to achieving the Programme's objective. This includes organisations representing or working with or on behalf of travellers and groups such as the homeless and long term unemployed.

438.   The Programme, which receives substantial support from the European Commission is the responsibility of the Department of the Taoiseach. The Departments of Enterprise and Employment, and Environment, and Area Development Management Limited implement the programme.

Back to Work Allowance

439.   This allowance was introduced in September, 1993 and is a specific incentive designed to encourage the long term unemployed to seek out employment. It provides a financial cushion to this disadvantaged group to help them re-enter the workforce and is administered by the Department of Social Welfare. Persons who take part in the scheme receive 75% of their weekly social welfare entitlement (including adult and child dependent allowances) in the first year, 50% for the second year and 25% for the third year. To date, over 10,000 have left the live register to take up this allowance. Almost two thirds are involved in self-employment. In 1996, the number of participants has been increased to 15,000 while an additional IR£150,000 has been provided to assist participants engaging in self-employment ventures with advice, technical assistance and relevant training. Funding for 1996, therefore totals IR£600,000.

PRSI Exemption Scheme

440.   This scheme exempts employers from their portion of Pay Related Social Insurance Contributions for up to two years where they increase employment over the level pertaining at the time of application and maintain that increase for the following two years. All first time job seekers under 23 are eligible even if they are not on the live register. The value of the subsidy is 12.2% of the employee's gross wage.

Community Employment Programme

441.   This programme was launched in 1994 and is a programme which offers an opportunity for work of value to individuals and to the community for those who

face a high risk of permanent unemployment in the open labour market. Its aims are to provide temporary work experience together with training for the long term unemployed and other special categories and to help voluntary groups and public sector bodies to do worthwhile work which they could not otherwise have undertaken. However, from April 1996, they will pay full-rate Pay Related Social Insurance contributions, thus being covered for all risks. The PRSI Exemption Scheme, outlined in Paragraph 440, will be available to Community Employment Sponsors to alleviate any additional costs arising on their side.

Local Employment Service

442. This service is based on a collaboration between local statutory, community and social partner organisations and is being introduced following a recommendation in the Interim Report of the Task Force on Long Term Unemployment. It is being phased in initially, beginning in 14 areas and will provide access for unemployed people, particularly the long term unemployed to the full range of employment options and will also provide a specialised career path planning service comprising of guidance, counselling access to training/education and placement in employment.

Second Level and Further Education

443. All persons over 21 years of age who are in receipt of unemployment payments for at least 12 months can pursue approved full-time or part-time education programmes of Post Leaving Certificate/Vocational preparation and Training Programmes without the loss of social welfare entitlements. This is to encourage those with little formal qualifications to return to second chance or vocational training.

Third Level Allowance Scheme

444. This scheme, introduced in 1990 allows persons over 23 who are in receipt of an unemployment payment for at least five months to pursue a third level course at under graduate level and continue to receive their unemployment payment. This is particularly geared at unemployed people who gain access to colleges and universities under the mature student options. In 1995, 2019 people were approved to partake in this scheme, including post graduates for the first time.

Youthreach

445. Youthreach is a programme under the European Union Social Guarantee aimed at those who have recently left school with no or low educational qualifications. It provides a mix of educational, training and work experience programmes tailored to the specific needs of the individual. The interventions can last for up to two years. Evaluations have shown a very positive attitude of participants to the Programme, with many social and personal benefits to participants even where participation does not lead to full time regular employment. It is aimed specifically at 15/17 year Olds

and is operated locally by FÁS and Vocational Educational Committees under the overall direction of the Departments of Enterprise and Employment, and Education.

Special Support Programme for Peace and Reconciliation

446.   In the aftermath of the cease-fire of August 1994 in Northern Ireland, the European Commission established a task force to look in to further ways of giving practical assistance to Northern Ireland and the border counties of Ireland. The Programme for Peace and Reconciliation was endorsed by the European Council at Essen in December 1994 and funding for a three year period of 300 million ECUs was approved. The Sub-Programme on Social Exclusion includes a measure designed to promote the inclusion of children and young people and has a total funding allocation of 2.833 million ECUs in Ireland and 16.835 million ECUs in Northern Ireland.

Pre-School Facilities

447.   In September 1994, the Minister for Education initiated a pilot scheme of free pre-school provision in eight areas of social disadvantage. The objectives of the project are to expose young children to an educational programme which would enhance their development and offset the effects of social disadvantage. In each case, 60 children aged 3 to 4 years are catered for in two sessions of 30 children each. Each project is staffed by 2 qualified teachers and 2 child-care assistants. Very favourable rates of grant toward start-up and running costs are provided.

448.   While Health Boards are not directly involved in the provision of pre-school services they do support services which cater for children who are regarded as being at risk or disadvantage.

449.   In 1992, the latest year for which statistics are available, the Health Boards gave grants totalling in the region of IR£1.6 million in respect of 330 centres which catered for approximately 8,900 children. Grants by boards were paid either direct to the centres concerned or through local community based groups.

450.   An important provision contained in the Child Care Act is the introduction of arrangements for the supervision and inspection of pre-school services. Certain provisions in respect of planning, fire safety standards and environmental hygiene regulations are applicable to creches, playschools and other pre-school facilities in the same manner as the other premises providing services for members of the public. However, Part VII (to be implemented by the end of 1996) of the Act now provides for the preparation of specific regulations governing their operation and the standard of care which they provide for the children using them.

451.   The Act empowers the Minister for Health, in consultation with the Ministers for Education and the Environment, to make regulations to secure the health, safety and welfare, and promote the development of, children attending pre-school services. Persons carrying on a pre-school service or proposing to do so will be required to

notify the relevant Health Board of their services. The Regulations will place on those providing pre-school services a statutory duty to take all reasonable measures to safeguard children using the services. Premises will be subject to inspection by the Health Boards and persons convicted of offenses under the Act will be subject to a fine or imprisonment or both.

452. The Government encourages the provision generally of childcare facilities through co-operative action by employers and employees and their respective organisations to enable parents fulfil their family and work responsibilities and in order to facilitate the integration of women into the workforce.

453. The Government is conscious of the contribution which childcare can make in promoting equal opportunities in employment. While the provision of childcare facilities is primarily a matter for parents, the Programme for Competitiveness and Work - agreed between Government and the Social Partners - undertakes to progress the development of facilities for working parents and those seeking education and training opportunities, to facilitate greater equality of access to such opportunities.

454. In this regard, over 70 projects located in areas of disadvantage have received assistance under a Pilot Childcare Initiative which was launched in 1994. Government funding in excess of £1 million has been issued to date in respect of this initiative. Under the scheme, grant assistance is available for initial start-up costs, such as the adaption of premises, purchase of equipment, cost of training etc., to enable local residents to undertake education, training, retraining and employment opportunities which they would otherwise be unable to aspire to in the absence of a child-care facility.

455. As an employer, the Government, through a number of its Public Sector Bodies and, in co-operation with the public service trade unions, has contributed to the provision of creche facilities for the children of its employees. An expansion of these facilities, to enable a greater number of state employees to avail of the service, is under active consideration.

VIII. EDUCATION, LEISURE AND CULTURAL ACTIVITIES

A. Education, including Vocational Training and Guidance (Art. 28), and Aims of Education (Art. 29)

456. Article 42.3.2 of the Constitution provides that it is the duty of the State to require that "children receive a certain minimum education, moral, intellectual and social".

457. In accordance with the School Attendance Act, 1926, attendance at full-time education is compulsory for all pupils between 6 and 15 years of age, although, in line with the recently-published White Paper on Education, the minimum school-leaving age will soon be raised to 16 years or the completion of three years of junior cycle education, whichever is later. Article 42.2 of the Constitution provides that "parents shall be free to provide this education in their homes". However, it is very unusual for parents to do so and where it is done the State is entitled to monitor the quality of the education provided.

458. Education services of a high standard are provided by the Irish State. However, a number of concerns were expressed in recent OECD and ESRI reports, in particular in relation to the percentage of students who leave the educational system without qualifications. The OECD Report estimated that some 6.6% of students left the education system without qualifications in 1991/2. The recent White Paper on Education seeks to tackle this problem by raising the minimum school leaving age from the current 15 years to 16 years. In addition, students must complete junior cycle education. The White Paper seeks to ensure as a major objective that the percentage of the 16-18 year old age-group completing senior cycle will increase to at least 90% by the year 2000.

459. The State currently provides for free education up to the age of 18 years in most second-level schools. While the role of the State in statutory schooling is specified in the Constitution, the expression of that role is in the context of an express or implied reservation in favour of the rights of parents. The Irish education system for first and second level schools is somewhat unusual in that the State provides financial assistance to the majority of schools, who, within the broad parameters set out by the Minister for Education, function as relatively autonomous bodies.

Primary Education

460. Article 42.4 of the Constitution reads as follows:

> "The State shall provide for free primary education and shall endeavour to supplement and give reasonable aid to private and corporate educational initiative, and, when the public good requires it, provide other educational facilities or institutions with due regard, however, for the rights of parents, especially in the matter of religious and moral formation."

461. In Ireland the primary education sector comprises national primary schools, special schools and non-aided private primary schools. Private primary schools are autonomous in ownership and administration, and there is no provision for the Department of Education to monitor the curriculum offered in such schools, although normally teachers in these establishments are fully qualified. There is no public funding for these schools, the costs of which are met by parents fees.

462. In 1975 a system of Boards of Management was established for primary schools, replacing management by an individual, usually a local clergyman. Boards are responsible for the day-to-day governing of the schools, subject to the regulations laid down by the Department of Education in the **Rules for National Schools** and in circular's and directives issued from time to time. Each school has a patron, usually a senior authority of the appropriate denomination. Reflecting the size of the various religious denominations, most patrons are from the Catholic Church with a significant number from the Church of Ireland (Anglican Communion/Protestant Episcopal Church) and other Protestant Churches. In multi-denominational schools, the patron is a committee constituted as a limited company.

463. A Jewish primary school was opened in Dublin in 1933. English is the teaching language of the school, although Hebrew is taught by visiting teachers to the school because of its religious importance; this aspect of the curriculum is under the general control of the Chief Rabbi of Ireland.

464. In 1990, a Muslim primary school was opened in Dublin and recognised by the Department of Education. There are approximately 100 pupils enrolled coming from a wide catchment area in Dublin. English is the language of instruction and Irish is also taught in the school. The teachers are Irish and Irish-trained but the Imam appoints qualified teachers of Arabic to teach in a pre-school and in the primary school.

465. Although compulsory education does not start until age 6 years, some 54% of Irish children aged 4 years and 99% aged 5 attend primary school.

466. As far as possible primary schools have single-grade classes. However, in smaller schools it may be necessary to combine class levels with one teacher. Generally speaking, pupils progress to the next grade at the end of the year, although exceptions do arise. There is no formal end-of-year examination.

467. Research has shown that the amount of time which students spend in organised learning activities has a critical bearing on their academic performance and all round development. A circular, **Time in School,** has recently been issued to all primary schools. It is designed to confirm the integrity of the school day and the school year and to ensure that pupils receive a minimum number of teaching hours per day and days per year.

468. Primary education is founded on the belief that high-quality education enables children to realise their potential as individuals and to live their lives to the fullest capacity as is appropriate to their particular stage of development.

469. In primary schools development education is accorded high priority. Teachers seek to cultivate attitudes of understanding and appreciation of how people live in the world today. This is being done in a formal way in religion, geography and history classes and in an informal way when dealing with current affairs issues.

The Pupil Teacher ratio in National Schools in 1993/94		
1	Total enrolment in all National Schools (September 30, 1993)	505,833
2	Total number of teachers in service (June 30, 1994)	20,776
3 = 1/2	Pupil Teacher Ratio in all National Schools	24.3
4	Total enrolment in Ordinary Classes	494,322
5	Teaching Teachers of Ordinary Classes	17,619
6 = 4/5	Average class size (Ordinary Classes)	28.1

470. While parents are free to choose schools for their children, factors such as geographic location in relation to a particular school and feasibility of travel may limit that choice. Children generally attend their local primary schools.

Remedial Education

471. Pupils in need of remedial education are those who experience clearly-observable difficulties in literacy and/or numeracy. Remedial teachers are appointed over and above the staffing quotas to schools of perceived need so that pupils can be given special tuition.

Home/School Community Liaison Scheme

472. There is also a Home/School/Community Liaison Scheme which began in 1990 in primary schools in designated areas of disadvantage and in 1991 in second-level schools. The aim of the scheme is to encourage active co-operation between home, school and community agencies in advancing the educational interests of the children.

473. Under the schemes, the schools have the service of a locally based coordinator who works with the pupils, their parents and the school to develop greater parental involvement in the education of their children.

Secondary Education

474. The second-level education sector in Ireland comprises secondary, vocational, community and comprehensive schools.

475. Education is free of charge in all schools financially maintained by the State (vocational schools/community colleges, comprehensive and community schools) and also in the majority of (independent) secondary schools provided by the voluntary sector which participate in the scheme of free education established in 1967. Approximately 7% of second-level schools charge fees.

476. In order to register in a second-level school, pupils must be aged 12 years on 1 January of their first year in second-level schooling. The first three years of second-level education are called junior cycle; senior cycle describes the two or three years in school after the junior cycle.

477. Although compulsory education ends at 15 years, an estimated 77% of pupils currently complete senior cycle (at age 18 approximately). As already stated, the target is for at least a 90% completion rate by the end of the 1990's.

478. The content of the curriculum is being addressed to ensure that gender bias is avoided at all levels of the educational system. Intervention projects in physics and chemistry and action to encourage girls to take up higher-level mathematics and technological subjects are ongoing at second-level. Teacher in-service courses have a mandatory module in gender equity.

Irish Language Education

479. All Primary and Post-Primary pupils are required to study Irish unless they are specifically exempted from doing so by the conditions of exemption drawn up by the Department, which are mainly concerned with pupils who have been partly educated abroad before enroling in a school in Ireland and pupils with particular learning disabilities.

480. In response to local demand, schools may be established in which pupils are educated through the medium of Irish. In recent decades, the number of these schools outside Irish speaking areas, the Gaeltacht, has been increasing and there are now 10,000 pupils enrolled. Extra financial and teaching resources are provided to these schools and each teacher receives a special annual allowance for teaching through Irish.

481. A daily grant per student is paid to Irish-speaking households providing accommodation for students attending Irish language courses in the Gaeltacht. Annual grants are also paid in the Gaeltacht areas to Irish-speaking households with school-going children.

Immigrant Pupils

482.   The small number of immigrant pupils and their wide residential scatter poses problems for the teaching of their mother tongue in schools in Ireland. Despite this, considerable provision is being made for such pupils. Most immigrant pupils acquire a knowledge of English through participation in classes at school and general community life. Most of these pupils also attend Irish language classes in their schools. A study completed in 1994 found that a total of 1,812 children of non-English speaking immigrants from European Union countries were at school in Ireland. The largest number (543) was German. Immigrants from 84 non EU countries accounted for a total of 2,311 pupils in primary and second-level; the largest group was Chinese (427).

Environmental Education/Information

483.   A public information service on the environment entitled "ENFO" was established in 1990. The objective of this service is to help protect and enhance the environment by promoting a wider understanding and fuller awareness of the natural world, particularly among children. ENFO provides information to the public in a variety of ways, including exhibitions and lectures, and its facilities include on-line access to international databases.

484.   ENFO also provides educational material for use by teachers in primary and post-primary schools. A resource pack on air quality has been produced and circulated to all schools and a similar pack on water is currently being produced. The ENFO library contains a number of other resource packs on environmental themes prepared by various agencies and these are made available on loan to teachers. ENFO is also extensively used by children undertaking school examinations or projects relating to environmental issues.

Psychological Service

485.   The Department of Education's Psychological Service, which initially served second-level pupils, and more recently, primary schools, was established in 1965. The service is responsible mainly for educational guidance and remedial provision. It has also developed and put in place several programmes in the area of health education. In its work in schools, the service combines individual case work with pupils with work with parents, teachers, whole staffs and local management. In addition, the psychologists link with other agencies providing services to schools in order to co-ordinate provision.

486.   The guidance service at second level, delivered mainly by the guidance counsellor, with the close co-operation of management, other teachers and parents, is made up of all the services, programmes and activities within the school which help students to a better understanding of themselves and their potential. The service includes assessment and appraisal of pupils abilities and aptitudes, the provision of information which helps

pupils to make informed decisions about educational, vocational and career choices, and counselling, which is available to all pupils as appropriate but especially those with special needs and those who have learning or personal difficulties.

School Attendance

487.   School attendance is monitored by School Attendance Officers in the three largest cities and the Garda Síochána elsewhere. Juvenile Liaison Officers are appointed from within the Garda Síochána and the Attendance Officers, parents and schools can call on their assistance in dealing with truancy. Under the current legislation penalties may be imposed on parents who fail to comply with the School Attendance Act. Employers who employ school-age children may also be fined.

488.   To increase the effectiveness of the system, a review of the operation of the School Attendance Acts, including an examination of the roles and responsibilities of the various agencies involved, was carried out by the Department of Education and the resulting School Attendance/Truancy Report was published in April, 1994. A Task Force in the Department of Education is currently considering recommendations to address the problem of school non-attendance at first and second levels.

School Discipline

489.   In 1982, the use of corporal punishment was abolished in Irish schools. Following this, a committee was established by the Minister to consider the question of discipline in schools and to make recommendations. As a result, Guidelines on Discipline were issued to school authorities and teachers in 1988, 1990 and 1991.

490.   In the Guidelines, all schools are strongly urged to formulate a code of discipline, to be drawn up by the principal and staff in consultation with parents and older pupils. A number of publications on this topic have also been produced.

491.   Arising out of the fact that corporal punishment is not permitted or practised in Irish schools, consideration is being given to the desirability of formally reflecting this position in the criminal law by removing any existing immunity which teachers may have from criminal prosecution for assaults on children. This is a recommendation of the Law Reform Commission in its report on Non-Fatal Offences Against the Person (LRC 45-1994) which is currently being examined with a view to the preparation of legislation.

492.   The Law Reform Commission also examined the common law immunity which permits parents and persons in loco parentis to use reasonable and moderate chastisement in the correction of their children. The Commission concluded that it would be premature to abolish this immunity immediately, but looked forward to a time when a process of re-education of parents would facilitate a change in the law.

Bullying

493.   A number of limited surveys (covering a sample size ranging from 700 to 1200) have been carried out to investigate the incidence of bullying within primary and post primary schools. The surveys are in broad agreement that a certain level of bullying does exist within Irish schools, with roughly 5-7% of students being bullied regularly, with 3-5% of pupils engaged in bullying. These figures appear to match the results of similar surveys in other European countries.

494.   One of the more interesting points to have emerged from these limited surveys is that the incidence of bullying has been found to be lowest where the school itself has an active policy and code of discipline on bullying. In 1993 the Department of Education issued a set of guidelines on bullying to all schools within the State. The aim of the guidelines was to increase the awareness of bullying behaviour in schools and to assist schools in devising school-based measures to prevent and deal with bullying behaviour.

Suspension and Expulsion

495.   The question of suspension and expulsion from school was considered by a working party which was set up to review the School Attendance Act, 1926. The School Attendance/Truancy Report, (April 1994) mentioned above, contains a number of relevant recommendations. The Report and comments on it from interested parties are under consideration at present.

496.   While school authorities may suspend, for a short period, seriously disruptive pupils or those guilty of serious breaches of discipline, the Rules for National Schools provide that a pupil shall not be struck off the rolls for breaches of discipline without the prior consent of the patron and unless alternative arrangements are made for the enrolment of the pupil at another suitable school.

497.   Where the Board of Management of a primary school deems it necessary to make provision in the code of discipline to deal with continuously disruptive pupils or with a serious breach of discipline by authorising the chairperson or principal to exclude a pupil or pupils from school, the maximum initial period of such exclusion may not exceed three school-days. A special decision of the Board of Management is necessary to authorize a further period of exclusion up to a maximum of ten school-days to allow for consultation with the pupil's parents or guardians. In exceptional circumstances, the Board may authorise a further period of exclusion in order to enable the matter to be reviewed.

498.   The "Guidelines Towards a Positive Policy for School Behaviour and Discipline" provide that expulsion should be resorted to only in the most extreme cases of indiscipline and only after every effort at rehabilitation has failed and every other sanction has been exhausted. Before any expulsion could take place considerable care would have to be taken in view of the Constitutional obligation to provide for free primary education.

Training

499.   The State Training and Employment Agency, FÁS, provides training for unemployed persons including young people under the age of 18 years who have left the education system and are seeking employment.

500.   The training provided for young people comes under the broad heading of initial training which encompasses a special measure for young people who have left school early with little or no educational qualifications and a scheme of apprenticeship training. The Early School Leaver measure provides up to two years integrated education, training and work experience for young people in the 15 to 18 age group. The programme is provided on an all year, full-time, 35 hours per week basis with a training allowance payable to participants. It is delivered in training centres specifically established to provide assistance for this group of young people. About 3,000 young people participate each year.

501.   Initial training is also provided via a formal apprenticeship system whose objective is to increase the supply of highly skilled crafts-persons in Ireland. A new standards-based system is being put in place which should be fully operational by the end of 1995. The recruitment of apprentices is a matter for employers but the new system requires that all apprentices spend 40 weeks off-the-job in a formal educational/ training establishment. It is estimated that about 3,500 apprentices will be recruited each year across a range of designated occupations.

Third-level Education

502.   Third-level educational institutions have expanded and developed considerably in Ireland since the mid 1960s. Student numbers have grown from 20,000 in 1965 to almost 90,000 in 1994 and it is foreseen that enrolments may be as high as 115,000 by the year 2000.

503.   Third-level education in Ireland is provided mainly by universities, technological colleges and colleges of education. A number of other institutions provide specialised training in such fields as art and design, medicine, theology, music and law. Most third-level education is provided in institutions that are supported by the State (e.g. universities and technological colleges receive more than 70% of their income from the State).

504.   Successive governments in Ireland have had as an important policy goal the availability of third-level education to all on the basis of capacity and substantial progress has been achieved in this area over the last number of years. A policy of providing easier access for more students has been pursued through the provision of additional places for students and the simplification of the entry process.

505.   In 1995, the Minister for Education announced the abolition of full time undergraduate third level tuition fees. In general the initiative applies to publicly funded third level

institutions. A further increase in the number of third-level places is also under consideration following the publication of a report on the future development of higher education in Ireland. Means-tested grant schemes are already provided for students in third-level institutions.

Prisons

506. The draft new Prison Rules (see paragraph 560) provide that special arrangements, including arrangements for enhanced education and training facilities, shall, as far as practicable, be made for the treatment of prisoners under 18 years of age.

507. At present education is available in all prisons and prisoners may attend, more or less, at will. At all institutions prisoners are made aware of the education facilities available by means of notices, information booklets and person to person contact.

Overseas Aid

508. Ireland supports a number of child-centred projects involving education. Particular emphasis is placed on teaching methodologies and materials designed to motivate and involve children in the learning process. The projects also aim to remove gender constraints in education.

B. Leisure, Recreation and Cultural Activities (Art.31)

Sport Policy

509. Sport policy in Ireland is based on the premise that every individual has a right to participate in sporting activities. Close co-operation and co-ordination between all sporting partners in developing and delivering a comprehensive range of sports programmes is strongly encouraged.

510. The Recreational Facilities Scheme and a Major Sports Capital Programme are administered by the Department of Education. The Recreational Facilities Scheme assists voluntary community organisations in the provision of community/ sports/youth facilities. A total of 500 projects have been assisted in 1994. The Major Sports Capital Programme was introduced by the Government in 1988 for the provision of regional and local sports centres at specified locations throughout the country. The programme now comprises up to 100 projects, with about 60 completed or under construction and the remainder at various planning stages.

Swimming Pools

511. Funding is provided to local authorities and voluntary bodies for the building of new swimming pools (80% grant-aid) and the refurbishment of existing pools (100% grant-aid) subject to compliance with specified standards. In addition, grants of up to 80%

of the cost of modest ancillary facilities may be provided. Small children's pools may be incorporated in such developments. A total of IR£2 million has been provided for the Swimming Pool Programme in 1995.

Youth Affairs

512. The Department of Education has a Youth Affairs Section which deals with youth issues outside the formal education sector. The task of this Section is to make informal educational services available to young people. This is principally done through the provision of financial assistance to special projects for disadvantaged young people and to national youth organisations.

513. The aim of the youth service is to assist all young people to become active participants in a democratic society. This participation, essential to the full development of young people, extends to involvement in institutions of social, political, cultural and economic life.

514. The Youth Affairs Section operates a grant scheme for projects to assist disadvantaged youth in respect of out-of-school projects. It also provides resources for the development of a network of youth information centres and for the operation of **Gaisce**(Deed of Valour), the President's Award Scheme. Finance is also made available for a variety of youth exchange programmes.

515. The White Paper on Education laid great stress on the importance of youth affairs. This is reflected in a number of initiatives which are due to be commenced shortly. A National Youth Advisory Committee is to be established, bringing together all government agencies involved in the delivery of youth services, together with a body representative of the youth organisations.

516. The Education Boards, which will be set up under forthcoming legislation, will be given statutory responsibility for the co-ordination and development of youth work. Each Board will draw up a Youth Work development plan, in conjunction with interested parties. The Boards will also employ a Youth Development Officer, to carry out these functions.

517. The Government has also committed itself to introduce a Youth Service Act to provide a statutory basis for developing youth work in Ireland.

Arts Council

518. In their recently published, Arts Plan for 1995-1997, the Arts Council lists one of its strategic objectives as being "to encourage real participation in the arts in terms of availability and access, with particular reference to young people, children and people with disabilities and taking account of social as well as geographical barriers".

519. The Council no longer regards provision for the education of young people and children as discrete and has restructured its operation to ensure a more integral approach, making education a central feature for all its work. The Council will accordingly strive to allocate 15% of its funding to young people and children from 1995, increasing it from its 1994 level of 6.5%. The Council recognises young people and children as a distinctive and active audience for whom the formal education system is but one point of access to the arts.

520. In order to meet this objective as far as children and young people are concerned, The Arts Plan provides that the Arts Council will work with the Youth Affairs Section of the Department of Education to implement **Making Youth Arts Work, 1993** - the report of the National Youth Arts Committee - which provides a blueprint for partnership to achieve increased participation for young people in the arts.

521. Programme development in music, drama, visual arts, dance and the youth services, being undertaken by the National Association for Youth Drama and the National Youth Council of Ireland, will receive continued support.

National Gallery

522. Each year, the National Gallery organises many activities for children and young people. Art workshops are held annually. In order to maximise the appeal of these workshops, the Gallery normally arranges for them to be given by some of Ireland's better known artists. Other events organised by the Gallery each year include school tours and the Schools Art Course - a series of lectures for teenagers based on the Junior and Leaving Certificate courses.

National Museum

523. The National Museum is also active in this area through its ongoing promotion of the museum as a resource for children. A stated priority of the National Museum, as part of its strategic development plan, is to enhance the educational experience of visitors as a whole, but particularly for children. A calender featuring Museum artifacts is circulated to every school in the country as a primary means of communication. In addition, when new exhibitions are being designed detailed consideration is given to the overall theme to ensure compatibility with young people and children.

The Ark

524. A new arts centre, **the Ark,** has recently been opened in Dublin. It is the first such centre in Europe to be designed, built and exclusively programmed for children. The Ark contains a theatre, gallery and workshop studio. The mission of the Ark is to promote and develop cultural work for children and by children.

IX. SPECIAL PROTECTION MEASURES

A. Children in Situations of Emergency

1. Refugee children (Art.22)

525. Ireland is a party to the 1951 UN Convention relating to the status of Refugees and to the 1967 Protocol to the Convention. Administrative proceedings agreed with the UNHCR for processing applications for refugee status do not discriminate against children. Children are treated equally in terms of the examination of their asylum claims and in terms of the rights they can enjoy if granted refugee status, subject to national provisions which apply generally to children. Ireland has not experienced the problem of unaccompanied children seeking asylum to any real extent.

526. Procedures to deal with applications for recognition of refugee status from unaccompanied children have been provided for in the Refugee Bill 1995. The rights of refugees who are recognised under the 1951 UN Convention and the rights of people included in the refugee resettlement programmes operated by the Government, are also dealt with in that Bill. In general, such refugees, including children where appropriate, enjoy the same rights as Irish citizens in the same circumstances. They may reside in the State, enter employment, carry on a business, have access to education, receive medical care and social welfare benefits and travel freely to and from the State. The implementation of proposals to put these arrangements on a statutory footing will further guarantee the equal treatment of applications, regardless of age.

527. Asylum seekers have tended to be adult males in the age bracket 1-35: the question of children asylum seekers arises in very few cases. Persons seeking asylum in this country generally arrive spontaneously. They arrive seeking refuge on the basis that they are fleeing from persecution in their home countries. Until 1993 the numbers seeking asylum in the country were relatively small - usually less than 50 per annum. As set out this has begun to change somewhat over the past couple of years with more asylum seeking families arriving here. It must be stressed that the numbers of children admitted are based on the numbers arriving. As Ireland is in a peripheral position on the edge of Europe with somewhat limited access routes this figure may be lower than for comparative countries.

Year	1991	1992	1993	1994	1995
Number of Asylum Seekers	31	39	91	355	424
Number of Children	n/a	n/a	n/a	25	35

Programme Refugees

528. As outlined in paragraphs 197-199 the Government operate two ongoing programmes for refugee resettlement in Ireland for groups of people from conflict areas. At present these programmes focus on Bosnian and Vietnamese people and operate in close cooperation with the UNHCR.

529. Requests for admission of unaccompanied children from emergency and conflict situations are rare and policy in such cases is guided by UNHCR principles, outlined in the UNHCR 1994 publication, "Refugee children - Guidelines on Protection and Care" and involves close cooperation with UNHCR. In recognition of the special needs of children in situation of emergencies, every effort is made to ensure that unaccompanied children are reunited with their parents and relatives as promptly as possible.

530. Since 1993 the Government have responded positively to the UNHCR appeal for treatment centres for seriously injured Bosnian's from the cities of Sarajevo and Tuzla. Five medical evacuations of injured groups from Sarajevo and Tuzla in Bosnia have taken place since 1993 in a response to the UNHCR appeal for treatment for seriously injured medical cases. To date a total of 55 medical evacuees are receiving treatment in Ireland of which two are children. Furthermore, the Government has substantially increased funding in the last two years for emergency assistance to victims of emergency conflict and natural disasters.

531. The Irish Government is committed to meeting the highest possible international standards with regard to the treatment of refugees. Ireland operates two ongoing resettlement programmes. These programmes allow for the admission to Ireland of persons who have fled their country of origin or normal residence because their lives, freedom or safety are threatened by violence or conflict. The decision to admit groups from conflict situations is taken by the Government on the advice of the Minister for Foreign Affairs. All Government decisions on the admission of such groups place particular importance on family reunification.

532. In recognition of the special needs which children have for a stable family environment, every effort is made to ensure that unaccompanied minors are reunited with their parents and relatives as quickly as possible.

533. There is also close co-operation between the Irish authorities and the UNHCR, which would extend to efforts to locate the parents of any refugee child were such a case to arise. If the parents could not be located, the child would be treated in all respects like any Irish child who is deprived of his or her family environment. Furthermore, the Irish Government recognise that it is implicit in any decision to admit a group of refugees that provision be made at a later stage to enable certain relatives to join them.

534. The **Refugee Agency** was established in 1991 and has the task of co-ordinating arrangements for the resettlement of groups of refugees who are admitted to Ireland

under Government Decision. The Agency operates under the aegis of the Department of Foreign Affairs and is administered by a Board which comprises representatives of Government Departments involved in issues related to refugee welfare and status (e.g. Justice, Social Welfare, Health, Education and Enterprise and Employment). The Board also includes representatives of the voluntary sector and the UNHCR. The Agency resettles refugees into privately rented accommodation and particular care is taken to preserve the integrity of families.

535.   The children of asylum seekers usually attend local schools and no particular difficulties exist as regards their schooling. Voluntary groups, such as the Irish Refugee Council, would also provide assistance in this area, e.g. by way of provision of language classes.

2.   Children in armed conflicts (Art.38), including physical and psychological recovery and social reintegration (Art. 39)

536.   The minimum ages of recruitment to the Defence Forces are 15 years for the Army School of Music, 16 years for apprentices and 17 years for all other entry categories, including the Air Corps and the Naval Service. There is no difference in the minimum ages of recruitment to the Defence Forces in times of emergency or conflict. However, persons under the age of 17 years can be recruited for specialist positions and must then undergo courses of specialist training. It is highly unlikely that such persons would be involved in operational situations.

537.   Children will have the status of protected persons in accordance with article 4 of the Fourth Geneva Convention relative to the Protection of Civilian Persons in Time of War. In addition, the provisions of articles 24, 25, 26 and 27 are designed to afford considerable protection to children in times of war. The Defence Forces are bound by the provisions of the Geneva Convention.

B.   Children in Conflict with the Law

1.   The administration of juvenile justice (Art.40)

538.   Article 15.5 of the Constitution declares that the Oireachtas shall not declare acts to be infringements of the law, which were not so at the date of their commission.

539.   Article 32.1 of the Constitution declare that no person shall be tried on any criminal charge save in due course of law. Every person, adult or child, is presumed under Irish law to be innocent until proven guilty.

540.   Regulations provide that an arrested person, adult or child, must be told in ordinary language of the offence or other matter in respect of which he or she has been arrested and that he or she is entitled to consult a solicitor. In addition, where an arrested person is under 17 years, a parent or guardian must be informed of the arrest, the

reason for the arrest and the right to consult a solicitor. The parent or guardian is also required to attend at the Garda station without delay.

541.   In criminal cases, free legal aid is granted by the Court, where the defendant, of whatever age, establishes to the satisfaction of the Court that his or her means are insufficient to pay for legal assistance and where the Court is satisfied that the gravity of the charge or exceptional circumstances make it essential in the interest of justice that the defendant should have legal aid in the preparation and conduct of his or her defence. The grant of legal aid entitles the defendant to the services of a solicitor (and in certain circumstances, counsel) in the preparation of his or her defence or appeal.

542.   Children charged with an offence have their cases tried in Courts established by law. Where the child is under 17 years, a special sitting of the District Court, known as a Children's Court or a Juvenile Court, hears the case, unless the offence is serious enough to be heard by a Court of higher jurisdiction.

543.   Where a person under 17 years is charged with any offence, under the Children Act, 1908 his or her parent/s must attend all stages of the proceedings unless he or she cannot be found or attendance would be unreasonable.

544.   No defendant in a criminal trial, adult or child, is required to give testimony or confess guilt. Every defendant is entitled to call witnesses on his or her behalf and to cross-examine opposing witnesses, either direct or through a solicitor or counsel.

545.   A conviction in the District Court may be appealed to the Circuit Criminal Court. A conviction in the Circuit Criminal Court or the Central Criminal Court (which hears the most serious categories of criminal cases) may be appealed to the Court of Criminal Appeal. A further appeal from the Court of Criminal Appeal to the Supreme Court may be made where the Court of Criminal Appeal or the Attorney General certifies that the decision involves a point of law of exceptional public importance and that it is desirable in the public interest that such an appeal should be taken.

546.   It is a fundamental principle of Irish law that a defendant must be in a position to understand the language used at the trial. Interpreters are provided if necessary, free of charge.

547.   It is not the practice of the media to publish any information concerning criminal trials which could lead to the identification of children involved in those proceedings. Consideration is currently being given to putting this on a statutory footing.

548.   The Juvenile Liaison Officer Scheme is an extra-statutory scheme introduced in the 1960's to divert young offenders from the judicial system. It provides for cautioning and supervising, as an alternative to prosecuting, juveniles who commit minor crimes. It is a requirement of the scheme that the juvenile admits the offence, and the parents or guardians agree to co-operate with the police in the implementation of the

Diversion Programme. While the consent of the victim is not a condition for inclusion in the scheme, any views expressed are taken into consideration.

549. The function of the Juvenile Liaison Officer is to maintain contact with any juvenile assigned to the JLO scheme, with the intention of weaning him or her away from involvement in crime. A juvenile who has or may have committed an offence and who has been warned, can be informally committed to the care of the Officer. The Juvenile Liaison Officer may also be entrusted with the care and guidance of a young person who, though not known to have committed an offence, may be regarded as a potential delinquent by reason of unsatisfactory behaviour, such as persistent truancy, running away from home, staying out late at night, being unruly at school or at home, behaving in a disorderly manner, or frequenting undesirable places. Such cases would come to notice through teachers, parents, school attendance officers, or the Gardaí generally.

550. The number of new cases (i.e. cautions) which came within the scope of the scheme in recent years is as follows:

1985	3,000	1990	3,180
1986	2,718	1991	4,508
1987	3,709	1992	5,271
1988	3,032	1993	5,526
1989	2,716		

551. Since the inception of the scheme in 1963, an annual aggregate of 89% of juveniles cautioned have not re-offended within their two-year supervisory period. There are currently 88 Juvenile Liaison Officers assigned to 38 major centres of population.

552. The Department of Justice recently announced the implementation of reforms to improve the effectiveness of the Juvenile Liaison Officer scheme and to ensure that this option is available for all suitable young offenders. A National Juvenile Liaison Office has been established to oversee the operation of this service throughout the State. The reporting and supervision arrangements for Juvenile Liaison Officers are being reformed with the Garda management at District Court level (generally Garda Superintendents) being given greater responsibilities in this area. There will also be a variation in the duration of the period of supervision by Juvenile Liaison Officers of their charges.

553. Examination of the issue showed that a more flexible approach was required in this area. In future, the approach will be more closely tailored to the needs of the young people concerned. Given the family situation of the young people involved in this scheme, the Garda Commissioner is of the view that there should be scope for members of the Juvenile Liaison Service to visit the young people under their supervision at a time when their parents are most likely to be available, i.e. in the evenings and at weekends. Juvenile Liaison Officers are now available to families at these times. Special training is also provided to Juvenile Liaison Officers.

554.   Apart from fines, courts have available to them the option of imposing probation orders and, for 16 and 17 year old offenders, community service orders. Consideration is currently being given to increasing the range of community-based sanctions and measures available to the courts.

2.   Children deprived of their liberty, including any form of detention, imprisonment or placement in custodial settings (Art. 37 (b), (c) and (d).

555.   No child can be deprived of his or her liberty except on foot of an order of a court imposing a sentence of detention or imprisonment. Any arrest, detention or imprisonment of a child must be in conformity with the law. Article 40.4 of the Irish Constitution provides that a judge of the High Court must enquire into any complaint of unlawful detention and must order the release of the person unless satisfied that the detention is in accordance with the law.

556.   The Department of Education has responsibility for the provision of residential accommodation for young male offenders up to 16 years of age and female offenders up to 17 years of age. There are currently five centres available for young offenders in Ireland. These can be divided into two categories, based on the age of the child and the seriousness of the offence. Generally speaking, industrial schools cater for children between 10 and 14 years of age, while reformatory schools cater for children between 14 and 16. The operation of these centres is currently governed by the 1908 Children's Act. New legislation is currently being prepared to replace this Act. While it is generally considered that there are an adequate number of industrial school places available, it is considered that further places are needed to provide for the older and more serious offenders.

Educational and Other Arrangements for Children in Care in Special Schools for Young Offenders on 30 June, 1994			
	Boys	Girls	Total
Number attending school on the premises:			
Primary..	111	13	124
Second-level..	72	—	72
Number in employment...	1	—	1
Other areas (Work Experience).............................	8	—	8
Total..	192	13	205

557.   In this context and in the light of recent Judicial and public concern the Government has decided to increase the available facilities through:

- the creation of additional industrial school places for girls and, ultimately, of a separate industrial school facility for girls, and

- the provision of additional reformatory school places and secure places for girls.

558. It is also planned to provide extra reformatory places for boys.

559. The Department of Justice has responsibility for the detention of male committals aged 16 years and over and females aged 17 years and over. Males under 16 and females under 17 cannot be sent to the prisons or places of detention operated by the Department of Justice (except in exceptional circumstances specified in Sections 97 and 102 of the Children Act 1908 where the Court certifies that the young person is of so unruly or depraved a character that he/she cannot be detained in a special school).

560. The 1947 Rules for the Government of Prisons classify every prisoner under the age of 17 years as a juvenile offender and make specific provision for these offenders. The Department of Justice has prepared draft new Prison Rules, which it is hoped will come into force as early as possible in 1996. The draft new Prison Rules provide for certain modifications to the general Prison Rules in the case of prisoners under 18 years, effectively extending the concept of juvenile offender to persons in that age category.

561. Offenders between 15 and 18 years of age, in common with all offenders in prisons/places of detention, have access to a range of counselling and psychological services. These are provided by doctors, psychiatrists, psychologists, probation and welfare officers, chaplains, teachers, workshop instructors, and by voluntary bodies such as Alcoholics Anonymous, Narcotics Anonymous, Gamblers Anonymous, and by The Samaritans who are available on a 24-hour, 365-day-a-year basis, by telephone.

Male inmates

562. Male offenders aged 16 to 21 years may be committed by the Courts to Saint Patrick's institution which is a place of detention for males in this age group. Males aged 17 years and over may also be sent by the Courts to the committal prisons: Mountjoy, Cork, Limerick and Portlaoise. The Department of Justice also has responsibility for the operation of places of detention which include institutions such as Wheatfield and Shanganagh Castle (an open centre catering for male offenders in the 16-21 age group) which were set up under the Prisons Act 1970 as alternatives to prisons "for the purpose of the rehabilitation of offenders".

563. The Minister for Justice made regulations in August 1990 which made it possible to transfer to Wheatfield boys aged 15 years who have been sentenced to imprisonment, having been found by a court to be unruly or depraved. Wheatfield provides a much more suitable environment for these boys, who can be accommodated in close

proximity to other youths in their mid-and late teens and kept away from older offenders to a greater extent than is possible in a prison such as Mountjoy. The regime and facilities in Wheatfield allow for emphasis on education and work training for young offenders than other custodial institutions in the system.

Female Inmates

564. The female prisons at Mountjoy and Limerick generally cater for females aged 17 and over. They can cater for under 17's only on committal by the Courts and on certification that they are too unruly to be sent to a special school. A very small number of such offenders (two or three) are committed in any one year.

565. The physical accommodation for female offenders is very limited. There is no separate facility for housing young female offenders who have been certified as unruly and committed to prison. The practice is therefore to provide such persons with a single cell and to arrange, as far as is possible, for their recreation separately from the adult inmates. In the case of Mountjoy Female Prison, juvenile inmates are assigned upon committal a special prison officer who remains assigned to them until their release.

566. Of the 2,317 persons in custody in institutions run by the Department of Justice on 13 June 1995, there were 2 persons in custody aged 15 years, 53 persons in custody aged 16 years and 95 persons in custody aged 17 years.(Of these 2 persons aged 15 years, 2 persons aged 16 years and 7 persons aged 17 years were in custody in a prison).

567. The draft new Prison Rules state that "as far as practicable, prisoners under the age of 18 years may be accommodated separately from adult prisoners". The saver is necessary to provide for situations where, exceptionally, complete separation is either unavoidable or undesirable (e.g. a single prisoner would effectively be in solitary confinement if not allowed to mix with others). It is not possible, however, to guarantee that they would always be separate.

568. The existing Rules for the Government of Prisons, 1947 (section 222(3)) also provide that juveniles (i.e. prisoners under the age of 17 years) who have not been in prison before and who are well-conducted in prison shall be kept separate from those who have been in prison before or who misbehave in prison. Section 224 also provides for the separation of juvenile offenders from adult offenders when taking exercise, receiving instruction and attending chapel.

569. Similar conditions apply to prisoners of all ages with regard to visits, letters and other communications. The existing arrangements for visiting is that in general each prisoner is entitled to at least one visit per week but, in practice, visits are allowed more frequently where circumstances permit. Visits in open centres are unsupervised and may be granted on demand. Phone calls are permitted exceptionally. Persons serving sentences are generally allowed to send two letters per week. Extra letters to family or a solicitor may be allowed on request. A prisoner awaiting trial may send out as many

letters as he or she likes. There is no limit to the number of letters which may be received.

570.   The juvenile justice system is at present governed in the main by the Children Act, 1908. The system is currently being reviewed with the intention of repealing the 1908 Act and replacing it with a comprehensive, modern statute which will deal with all aspects of juvenile justice.

3.   The sentencing of juveniles, in particular the prohibition of capital punishment and life imprisonment (Art. 37 (a))

571.   No Court in Ireland may pass a sentence of capital punishment. The death penalty was abolished by the Criminal Justice Act, 1990. Ireland has also ratified the Second Optional Protocol to the International Covenant on Civil and Political Rights.

572.   The possibility of early release exists for every person, of whatever age, sentenced to life imprisonment. The Minister for Justice may authorise the release of any prisoner prior to the completion of his or her sentence. In addition, all prisoners who have served seven years or more of a current sentence may, if they so wish, have their sentences reviewed by an independent Sentence Review Group. The Group advises the Minister on the administration of long sentences and may recommend early release. In the event that early release is not recommended, there is provision for subsequent reviews at regular intervals.

4.   Physical and psychological recovery and social reintegration (Art. 39)

573.   In Ireland, the Departments of Education, Justice and Health liaise closely in the provision of support services targeted on children in conflict with the law.

574.   The Department of Education has responsibility for the operation of five Young Offenders Centres which cater for the detention of young persons committed by the Courts. Accommodation in these centres is comprised of short-term remand facilities and long-term detention facilities. The operation of the centres is governed by the provisions of the Children Act, 1908. The long-term facilities are certified by the Minister for Education and the remand facility by the Minister for Justice. The centres are funded by the Department of Education and operate under the overall control of the Department.

575.   The primary role of the centres is to provide a programme of care and education aimed at rehabilitating those referred to them by the Courts. Boys and girls up to 17 years of age on the date of admission are catered for.

C. Children in Situations of Exploitation, including Physical Recovery and Social Re-integration (Art. 39)

1. Economic exploitation, including child labour (Art.32)

576. The Protection of Young Persons (Employment) Act, 1977 provides legislative protection for young workers under the age of 18 years. It contains provisions concerning the minimum age for entry into employment, sets limits to the working hours of young people, provides for rest intervals and places restrictions on night work. It also requires employers to keep records of the ages and working times of employees under 18 years of age.

577. The employment of children under the school leaving age, which is presently 15 years, is generally prohibited. However, a child over 14 years, but under the school leaving age, may be permitted to do light non-industrial work during school holidays, provided that it is not harmful to the child's health or normal development and does not interfere with his or her schooling. Such children may not be employed during school term, with the exception of second-level students participating in work experience or other similar educational courses arranged or approved by the Minister for Education.

578. The protection of Young Persons (Employment) Act, 1977 allows the Minister for Enterprise and Employment to grant exemptions from provisions of the Act by way of licence. A licence was issued in June 1994 permitting the employment of children in the film production industry, subject to very stringent conditions, including restrictions on hours of attendance, rehearsal and performance. The licence also provides specific conditions on chaperones and safety, health and welfare conditions.

579. The working hours of a child under 15 years during school holidays shall not exceed 7 hours in any day, 35 hours in any week. During school summer holidays, he or she must not do any work for one full period of 14 days. The employment of children under school leaving age is prohibited for a period of 14 consecutive hours at night including the interval between 8 p.m. and 8 a.m.

580. Young persons between the ages of 15 and 18 years are not permitted to work for a period of 12 consecutive hours at night including the period between 10 p.m. on one day and 6 a.m. on the following day. Such persons employed on industrial work must not be employed between the hours of 8 p.m. on one day and 8 a.m. on the following day.

581. Young persons under 18 years of age are entitled to 30 minute rest intervals which, in the case of an employee who is aged between 15 years and 18 years, must be given after 5 hours' work and, in the case of those under 15 years, must be given after 4 hours' work. A rest period of 30 minutes must also be provided before any period of overtime in excess of 1½ hours is worked.

582.   Before an employer employs anyone under 18 years, he or she must first require the production of that person's birth certificate. In addition, before employing a child aged 14 to 15 years, written permission must be obtained by the employer from the child's parent or guardian.

583.   The Intoxicating Liquor Act, 1988 provides that, in general, young persons under 18 years of age may not be employed in any premises licensed for the sale of intoxicating liquor. The only exceptions are close relations of the licence holder and apprentices, where they reside with the licence holder and are not under 16 years of age.

584.   Compliance with the Protection of Young Persons (Employment) Act, 1977 is supervised by the Labour Inspectorate and any breaches of the legislation are punishable by fines.

585.   Proceedings in relation to an offence under the Act may be brought by the Minister for Enterprise and Employment, by the trade union concerned or by the employee's parent or guardian.

586.   The Safety, Health and Welfare at Work Act, 1989 imposes a general duty of care on employers in relation to all employees. The provisions of the 1989 Act are amplified by the Safety, Health and Welfare at Work (General Application) Regulations 1993. The 1993 Regulations also impose a particular duty on employers to ensure that particularly sensitive risk groups of employees, which would include children, are protected against any dangers which specifically affect them.

587.   The statutory provisions governing the protection of young persons in employment are currently being reviewed in the context of the need for implementation of an EU Directive on the Protection of Young People at Work. While the Directive is in many respects similar to the existing Protection of Young Persons (Employment) Act, 1977 there are some differences which will be required to be enshrined in the new laws giving effect to the terms of the Directive. One of the principal differences is that the Directive imposes some specific health and safety responsibilities on the employers of young persons. Under the Directive, employers are required to carry out risk assessments in relation to young persons in the workplace and young persons are prohibited from work-places which have specific risks. These obligations are more specific than the current obligations under the Safety, Health and Welfare at Work Act, 1989.

588.   In giving effect to the terms of the Directive, there will be widespread consultation with the various interested parties in advance of the June 1996 deadline for implementation of the Directive.

2.   Drug misuse (Art. 33)

589.   The Government published a comprehensive strategy in 1991, which is designed to protect all persons, including children, from the dangers of drug misuse. The Strategy recognises that the problem of drug misuse is a complex and difficult one. It proposes a multidisciplinary approach requiring action in the areas of supply reduction, demand reduction and increased access to treatment and rehabilitation programmes, together with co-ordination mechanisms geared towards their effective implementation. The Strategy, while recognising the validity of a multiplicity of treatment and prevention programmes, advocates a drug-free lifestyle as the ideal. It also recognises, however, that various drug treatment options are required to deal with the needs of individual drug abusers. Such options include methadone maintenance, needle exchange, detoxification and rehabilitation.

Extent of the Drug Misuse Problem

590.   There is no accurate figure available for the number of drug misusers in Ireland. A report produced recently by the Health Research Board indicated that, in 1993, an estimated 2,573 people received treatment for drug misuse in the greater Dublin area. It must be emphasised that this is an estimate of the number of people receiving treatment rather than the number of people misusing drugs. It is accepted that the number of drug misusers is greatly in excess of this figure.

591.   The main points of the report included the following:

   •   Three quarters of the clients were male;

   •   1% of clients were under 15 years of age and 30% were between the ages of 15 and 20 years;

   •   Eight out of ten were unemployed;

   •   Almost four out of ten had left school before the official school leaving age of 15;

592.   Since 1992 special funding has been allocated each year to allow for the development of extensive prevention and treatment services in the Dublin area, where the majority of drug misusers reside.

593.   Support to families of young drug misusers is provided in each regional Health Board through the Community Addiction Service. Funding is also provided to a number of voluntary agencies which provide family counselling, advice and support. These include Coolmine Therapeutic Community, Mater Dei Counselling Centre, Community Awareness of Drugs and the Talbot Centre.

594.   Outside of Dublin, misuse of drugs is on a lesser scale and there is no evidence to suggest that intravenous drug misuse constitutes a serious problem. Those who do present for treatment do so because of problems with poly-substance abuse i.e. involving alcohol with cannabis, ecstasy and benzodiazepine. Each Health Board closely monitors the situation in order to be in a position to deal quickly with problems as they arise.

595.   The publication in 1992 of the recommendations of the National AIDS Strategy Committee has had a major impact on drugs policy, given the close connection between HIV/AIDS and intravenous drug misuse. At present, 57% of all known HIV positive cases in Ireland are drug-misuse related and the emphasis has been on putting in place a comprehensive treatment network for drug misusers.

596.   Since 1992, special funding has been allocated to allow for the development of extensive prevention and treatment services by the statutory agencies working in close collaboration with voluntary agencies.

597.   The ultimate objective of the treatment and rehabilitation programmes is a drug-free lifestyle. It is acknowledged, however, that this is not always an option for many drug misusers, at least in the initial stages of treatment, and consequently it has been necessary to introduce methadone maintenance programmes in community-based satellite clinics as a means of stabilising the behaviour of drug misusers and preventing HIV through sharing contaminated needles.

598.   The development of satellite clinics was recommended by the National AIDS Strategy Committee (1992) as a means of providing primary care services to drug users. These services are designed to prevent HIV-negative drug users from contracting the disease and HIV positive drug users from transmitting HIV to others. Other services provided by the clinics include counselling, risk reduction (needle exchange, free condoms etc.) and HIV testing.

599.   Section 74 of the Child Care Act, 1991, which was implemented in December 1991, makes it an offence to sell solvent-based products to children where it is known or suspected that they will be misused. It also gives a Garda power to seize any substance in the possession of a child in a public place which the Garda has reasonable cause to believe is being misused by that child in a manner likely to cause him or her to be intoxicated. See paragraph 79.

Drug Misuse Prevention.

600.   The Government Strategy to Prevent Drug Misuse recommended the establishment of a number of prevention programmes, both in the public sector and the voluntary sector. A substance abuse prevention programme is available to all second level schools and training in drug and solvent abuse prevention is offered to youth leaders and trainers. Financial support has also been given to a number of voluntary groups

working with young people in disadvantaged areas to discourage involvement in drug taking.

601.   A special programme has been developed for use with parents, helping them to deal with the problems of adolescence and drug misuse.

602.   Ireland also participates in European Drug Prevention Week (EDPW) which took place in 1992 and 1994, where the focus was on the prevention of drug misuse among young people. A comprehensive evaluation of the Week is being conducted by the EU to determine when the next EDPW will take place.

3.   Sexual exploitation and sexual abuse (Art. 34)

603.   It is an offence for a man to have sexual intercourse with a female under 17 years unless he is married to her. It is an offence for a man to take part in a homosexual act with a male under 17 years. Soliciting or importuning a person under 17 years for the purposes of committing any of these acts is also an offence. In addition, consent is no defence to a charge of sexual assault on a person, male or female, under 15 years.

604.   In addition to the general prohibition on sexual relations with under-age persons, there are comprehensive sanctions against the exploitation of persons through the organisation of prostitution.

605.   The use of a child in pornographic performances or materials may constitute an offence at common law. In addition while legislation on pornography is not specifically designed to deal with the protection of children from sexual abuse or exploitation by being portrayed in pornographic performances or material, it does provide mechanisms for the censorship of films and video works (and also written publications) which may be considered unsuitable for general circulation in the State by reason of indecency or obscenity. These measures have already been documented with regard to Article 17.

606.   Arising out of concern regarding sex tourism and the sexual exploitation of children in particular a Bill entitled the Sexual Offences (Jurisdiction) Bill is currently being considered by the Oireachtas. Its purpose is to extend the criminal law of the State to acts against children committed elsewhere by citizens of the State or by persons ordinarily resident within the State, but which if committed in this State would constitute a sexual offence. Another Bill which has recently been published by a member of the Oireachtas seeks to prohibit the organisation or promotion of child sex tourism.

4.   Other forms of exploitation (Art. 36)

607.   Reference is made to chapters VI (I) and IX (C).

5.   Sale, trafficking and abduction (Art. 35)

608.   Reference is made to chapter VI (H).

D.   Children Belonging to a Minority or an Indigenous group (Art. 30)

609.   A significant number of people belong to the Travelling Community in Ireland. This is a community whose members, like the gypsies in other countries, used to travel from place to place in pursuit of traditional callings. Many of these occupations have now become obsolete. Nowadays many Travellers tend to live close to the major cities. Some of the bodies representing Travellers claim that members of the Community constitute a distinct ethnic group. Members of the Travelling Community are protected by the Convention irrespective of membership of any ethnic group. The principle of non-discrimination is an integral part of this Convention and is welcomed by the Government. As far as discrimination against Travellers by private individuals is concerned, the Government has drafted the law in relation to incitement to hatred to cover incitement to hatred against Travellers.

Task force on the Travelling Community

610.   The Minister for Equality and Law Reform established a Task force on the Travelling Community to assist him in discharging his responsibility for articulating Government policy in relation to travellers. The Terms of Reference of the Task Force, which was set up in July 1993, included reporting to and advising the Minister on the needs of travellers, and government policy generally in relation to travellers, in a range of areas such as accommodation, health, equality, education and training.

611.   The Task Force issued an interim report in January 1994. Its final report was published on 20 July 1995. The report was the first comprehensive review of the needs of the Travelling Community since the Report of the Travelling People Review Body published in 1983. The publication of the report comes at a time when the needs of travellers and their relationship with the settled community are the subject of public debate particularly in regard to the question of accommodation.

612.   The report of the Task Force examines, and makes recommendations in relation to, three principal areas, namely:

- key issues of relevance to Travellers including accommodation, access to health services, education and training provision and economic development and employment including the co-ordination of approaches by the relevant statutory agencies whose services impact on members of the traveller community;

- relationships between Travellers and the settled community;

- the experience of Travellers with a particular focus on culture and discrimination.

Many of the recommendations in the Report of the Task Force also cover services provided to Traveller children e.g. education, health, discrimination, accommodation.

613. The main elements of the recommendations put forward by the Task Force include:

- the need to provide 3,100 units of additional accommodation by the year 2000, with supporting administrative and legislative changes;

- the introduction of measures to improve the health status of the Travelling Community and to remove the obstacles to Traveller access to the health services;

- the re-organisation and development of the education services in order to provide for increased participation levels by Travellers;

- the encouragement and undertaking of new initiatives to support the development of the Traveller economy and increased levels of Traveller participation in the mainstream labour force;

- the adoption of measures which address the problem of discrimination faced by the Travelling Community;

- the introduction of and/or, where necessary, the improvement of mechanisms in order to ensure that statutory agencies which provide services that impact on Travellers do so in a coordinated manner;

- the need to increase participation by Travellers and Traveller organisations in the decision making process in areas which affect Traveller's lifestyle and environment.

614. The Report also examines mechanisms for facilitating improved relationships between the traveller and settled communities, particularly at local level and make recommendations with a view to reducing conflict and strengthening mutual respect and understanding which it is hoped will merge into, what the Task Force calls, a Strategy for Reconciliation.

615. As the report of the Task Force impacts on a wide range of policy areas which are the responsibility of a number of Ministers, the Irish Government has established an inter-Departmental working group of officials to consider the implementation of the Report, including in particular, the costs involved. The Government will determine what action is called for in relation to the recommendations contained in the Task Force Report as soon as the report of the working group is available.

Accommodation

616.   Local authorities are responsible for the provision of halting sites (serviced caravan parks) for Traveller families. There are approximately 4,000 Traveller families (about 25,000-30,000 people) in the State, of whom about 2,900 are in local authority accommodation in housing or on halting sites. Government policy is that Traveller families should be accommodated in the accommodation of their choice, whether housing or halting sites, and local authorities are constantly urged to meet their responsibilities in this regard. However, some Travellers are living in caravans on unofficial, unserviced sites and by the roadside and consequently endure harsh living conditions which can lead to health, educational and other difficulties.

Education

617.   The statistics for enrolment and school attendance among Traveller children have improved significantly in recent years. There are 5,000 Traveller children of primary school age or younger in Ireland and it is now estimated that approximately 4,600 of these (92%) attend either pre-school or primary school. However, very few Travellers attend secondary school.

618.   The Government is seeking to develop further the educational service for Traveller children at pre-school, primary and second levels to ensure the participation of the children not attending at present and to seek the maximum possible integration of Traveller children into ordinary schools.

619.   At pre-school level, 55 schools with an approximate enrolment of 660, located adjacent to halting sites, provide special preparation for the children before enrolment in primary schools. The State provides almost the total costs of these pre-schools which were established by voluntary bodies. The aim is to provide children with basic skills in literacy, numeracy and social behaviour in preparation for primary school.

620.   During 1994, a booklet entitled **The Education of Traveller Children in National Schools: Guidelines**, outlining strategies for integrating Travellers into the primary school system, was issued to all primary schools. Significant success has already been achieved as approximately 4,000 children of Travellers, some of whom are over 12 years of age, attend mainstream classes. Where full integration is not immediately possible, special classes are provided to enable Traveller children to prepare for such integration.

621.   Special measures at primary school level include the provision of extra funding and almost 200 extra teachers to schools enroling Traveller children and the development of reading materials for use with these children.

622.	The objective at second-level is to integrate Traveller children into mainstream education. In the interim, the Department of Education is supporting 11 Junior Training Centres which cater for Traveller children in the 12-15 age group. These centres aim to provide a form of second-level education for Traveller children sufficiently relevant and attractive to encourage them to continue attending school.

623.	A visiting teacher service for Travellers, consisting at present of 12 visiting teachers, provides special support for children attending ordinary primary schools by calling to the schools and families, liaising with Health Boards and voluntary agencies and encouraging participation in the education system. It is also intended to appoint visiting teachers at second level. In addition, a National Education Officer for Travellers has responsibility for co-ordinating the education of Travellers in all areas and at all levels. Further development of the provision for Traveller children, particularly at second level, is planned.

624.	Training of Travellers of 15 years of age and over is provided through a network of Traveller training centres managed by locally based management committees and jointly funded by FÁS (the State Training and Employment Authority) and Vocational Education Committees. The goal of the training centres is to help Travellers develop their full potential and to enable them to become self-reliant and self-supporting members of society. Training is provided for 48 weeks during which a training allowance is paid to participants and around 600 attend the centres each year.

Health Services

625.	The same health services are available to the Travelling Community as to the settled population. However, special efforts are made to successfully deliver these services and to ensure that they are tailored to meet the specific needs of Travellers. Factors such as transient lifestyle, large families, high unemployment and generally poor health awareness are taken into account in the planning and delivery of health services to travellers. Every effort is made to encourage members of the Travelling Community to make maximum use of the services available.

626.	The infant mortality rate among the Travelling Community is more than twice the rate in the settled community. In 1987 the infant mortality rate per 1,000 live births was 7.4 for the settled community compared to 18.1 for the Travelling Community. Mortality rates are higher for Travellers than for the settled population. Life expectancy is considerably lower for Travellers than for settled people.

Child Care Services

627.	Child care support services for Traveller families are provided by social workers employed by both Health Board and local housing authorities. Amongst the services provided are pre-school services for young children. Developments under the Child Care Act contain specific measures to address the special needs of the Travelling Community.

628. The Eastern Health Board is involved in a number of services aimed at assisting Travelling children and their families as follows:-

- The Board in conjunction with the Department of Education, supports a school and preschool for 75 Traveller children at Saint Columba's Day Care Centre in Dublin. Children are collected each day and brought to school where meals, health care and other back-up services are available;

- The Board supports a resource centre operated by the Dublin Committee for Travelling People which provides amongst other services, an after-school and youth programme.

- The Board also provides financial assistance to the Dublin Committee for Travelling People towards the operating costs of two residential centres for Travelling children. These are located at Derralossary in County Wicklow and Ballyowen Meadows in Clondalkin which is accessible to the large numbers of Travelling families in West County Dublin.

Aftercare

629. An aftercare programme for young members of the Travelling Community leaving residential care has been developed and a special foster care placement programme is being developed by the Eastern Health Board whereby Traveller Families will become foster parents for both long term and short term placements, thus enabling the children to be cared for within their own communities.

X. CONSULTATION WITH THE NGO SECTOR

A. INTRODUCTION

630.   Recognising the important role that the NGO sector plays in matters concerning children, the Department of Foreign Affairs, in the drafting of this report, consulted formally and informally with a representative cross section of the NGO sector interested in the welfare of children.

631.   The purpose of the process of consultation was threefold:

- to ensure that Ireland's first report was an accurate reflection of the current status of the implementation in Ireland of the United Nations Convention on the Rights of the Child;

- to pinpoint the key concerns of the NGO sector and to afford them a meaningful opportunity to present to government officials their ideas on how Ireland could achieve fuller implementation of the United Nations Convention on the Rights of the Child;

- to explore the implementation by Ireland of the United Nations Convention on the Rights of the Child from an alternative perspective and to record this in a specific chapter in this report;

632.   On 16 November, 1995 a consultative meeting was held between five Government Departments involved in the drafting of Ireland's first report and a group of NGOs led by the Children's Rights Alliance, an umbrella body with more than 50 constituent members. Prior to the meeting the representatives of the Alliance were furnished with copies of the draft report on a confidential basis; it was hoped that this would lead to constructive deliberation and allow concerns to be shared from an informed position. The meeting did not set out to achieve agreement or consensus but rather to allow for a constructive exchange of views on the report.

633.   On 24 November, 1995 a meeting was held between two Government Departments and the Irish Commission for Justice and Peace regarding Ireland's first report. The meeting focussed in particular on conditions of detention for children.

634.   During the preparation of this report the Department of Foreign Affairs received for its consideration a document entitled "A Blueprint for Children" and a proposed submission to the UN Committee on the Rights Of the Child from Focus on Children, a cross-border umbrella body of children's organisations.

635.   Some of the key concerns of the NGO sector are outlined in the following paragraphs which are not an exhaustive analysis of all the concerns expressed but illustrate some of the issues which have arisen during the drafting of this report:

B.   GENERAL MEASURES OF IMPLEMENTATION.

636.   It was considered that there was insufficient statistical analysis and information available in Ireland on the needs of children which makes it difficult to respond adequately to those needs. Statistical information was viewed as necessary to facilitate an ongoing evaluation of the position of children and of the resources expended on children's issues, to ensure that the best possible use is made of those resources. A perceived lack of statistical analysis was a consistent theme throughout the consultative process. The Department of Health advised that such analysis was now underway in the context of its Health Strategy.

637.   Some representatives of the NGO sector raised the Constitutional position of children; Articles 41.1.1 and 42.1.4 of the Constitution could be said to imply a potential for conflict between children and parents given the constitutional focus on the rights of the latter.

638.   It was suggested that there was insufficient organisation between government departments and also between government and non-governmental sectors; improved coordination would enhance the provision of services for children.

639.   Concern was expressed at inadequate efforts designed to make children and adults aware of the terms of the Convention as required under article 42.

C.   DEFINITION OF THE CHILD

640.   It was suggested that as the age of majority in Ireland varies depending on circumstances, all Irish legislation should be aligned with the benchmark age of 18 years used by the Convention to define a child.

D.   GENERAL PRINCIPLES

641.   In the context of Article 2, the provision against discrimination, it was felt that the standard of care might vary too much from one Health Board area to another and that while acknowledging that treatment has to meet local needs, there should be agreement on key principles within the context of a national plan relating to the care and protection of children.

642.   The question of a national policy guaranteeing the rights of Irish speaking children to protect such children from discriminatory treatment was raised by an NGO representative. The provision of documentation in Irish was also addressed. Departments responded by indicating how they dealt with the needs of Irish speakers particularly in areas where there are substantial numbers of Irish speakers.

E.   CIVIL RIGHTS AND FREEDOMS

643.   It was suggested by an NGO representative that the legislation relating to the registration of birth was contrary to the provisions of the Convention because it did not require the registration of the father's name. It was argued that this was a denial of a child's right to know its parents.

F.   FAMILY ENVIRONMENT AND ALTERNATIVE CARE

644.   Concern was expressed at what was perceived as a delay in some rural areas in cases involving child custody and access. Such delays could result in a denial of the rights of a child to see one or both parents.

Adoption

645.   The legal necessity for a parent to adopt his or her own child, when a spouse of that parent (who is not a parent of that child) wishes to adopt that child, was cited as undesirable. The situation whereby adopted children do not have unrestricted access to the identity of their natural parents was pointed to as a possible violation of their rights under the Convention by a representative of the NGO sector.

Child Protection

646.   The issue of child protection was discussed in some detail. The work done to date in this area by the Government was recognised but areas where it was felt the full protection of the Convention was not being extended to children were identified.

647.   While the Child Care Act, 1991 provides for consultation with children the NGO representative believed that there is little evidence that such consultation takes place, particularly in case conferences where care proceedings are involved. It was emphasised that it is becoming more urgent to fully finance the implementation of all provisions of the Child Care Act, 1991.

648.   It was also suggested that there are a number of lacunae both in the way the Health Boards are administered and in the way the community itself responds to child protection issues. These were identified as, inter alia,

- Poor inter-agency work in some areas;
- Lack of clear decision making processes in cases of neglect and abuse;
- Unrealistic expectations in relation to workloads of those involved in child protection;
- Gaps in information, skills and supervision of "frontline workers";
- A lack of awareness of guidelines and procedures;
- A community mentality which may result in a distaste for reporting on others;

- A lack of confidence, following a report of abuse, in the outcome for the child and family given the emphasis on investigation with relatively little energy being given to subsequent support and treatment.

G.   BASIC HEALTH AND WELFARE

Social Security.

649.   It was submitted that Article 27(1) which recognises the right to an adequate standard of living for all children was central to the whole Convention and that if this right is not satisfied it has the consequent effect of restricting education and job opportunities; furthermore unemployment hinders a parent's ability to secure the conditions of living necessary for children's development. NGOs recognised the positive aspects of policy formulation and implementation in this area.

650.   Advances were also noted in tackling the problem of homelessness but it was pointed out that there were still problems, particularly for single parent families or families in refuge accommodation. Concern was expressed that the effects of long term unemployment, poverty and social exclusion were dealt with in a symptomatic way rather than by identifying and addressing the root causes.

Health

651.   NGOs commended the many positive aspects of the Health Service reflected in the Government report but outlined areas where Ireland may be falling short of its obligations under the Convention. They emphasised the lack of adequate guidelines and statistical analysis to assess the suitability of services available and suggested that this poses great problems for policy planning.

652.   It was also suggested that:

- there is a lack of cohesion between the primary, secondary and tertiary health services whose tendency to operate independently hinders the effective provision of care for children.

- inequalities associated with the existence of a private and public health service frequently result in lengthy waiting lists in the public sector.

- the provision of special training for those people dealing with children should be addressed and in particular the need for the provision of child psychologists.

- The needs of young children at an early verbal stage to communicate through the medium of play are not being met and this is reflected in a lack of hospital play specialists.

H. EDUCATION, LEISURE AND CULTURAL ACTIVITIES

653. The concerns expressed in respect of educational provision fell into two categories. The first category was resource oriented. Concerns focussed on the need to ensure that all aspects of primary and secondary education are free. Extra resources for Remedial Teaching were called for. Free third level education was also urged. The Department of Education advised that the continuing decline in the enrolments at primary level provides an opportunity to reduce the Pupil Teacher ratio generally, and to channel extra resources into the areas of special needs, including amongst others, remedial teachers. Furthermore, in addition to the abolition of third level fees, government policy, within overall resource constraints, is to increase the grants being provided to third level students, to reduce the associated costs of attending third level education.

654. The second category included the current system of school suspensions and expulsions and it was suggested that they may be contrary to children's rights under the Convention where repeated suspensions were in effect a form of expulsion. The problem of repeated suspensions is being addressed in the current review of the School Attendance Act.

655. Concern was also expressed at a perceived lack of consultation between schools and their pupils. A child's right to participate in decisions affecting them implies consultation procedures in educational bodies. The White Paper seeks to address this issue by encouraging Boards of Management in second level schools to promote the formation of a students' council, which will work in collaboration with the staff and parents' association.

I. SPECIAL PROTECTION MEASURES

Refugees

656. The situation of refugee children was the subject of some concern. Among the points mentioned were the provision of facilities to trace relatives, interpretation facilities, the issue of legal representation to assist applicants for legal status, and the long time limits to allow a person with refugee status to join his or her family.

Children in conflict with the Law

657. Concern was also expressed at the situation regarding children who found themselves in conflict with the law. The questions of deprivation of liberty and ensuring due process of law for children were addressed. The issues raised included the question of raising of the age of criminal responsibility which was an issue under consideration by the Government in the context of new legislation.

658. Concern was expressed regarding the detention of offenders less than 17 years of age and it was suggested that this was a matter for review as detention might be an

inappropriate response to such behaviour; a community-based response may be more appropriate for juvenile offenders. The view was also expressed that more information and statistical analysis are necessary to properly evaluate the system as well as improving coordination on all areas of juvenile detention.

659. Government officials responded by expressing the view that the creation of the coordinating committee on children's affairs under the Minister of State at the Departments of Health, Education and Justice would lead to greater cohesion in the area of juvenile justice. It was also hoped that a new bill being drafted in this area would address many of the concerns outlined by the NGOs.

Documents supplied with this Report to the UN Committee on the Rights of the Child

A. Legislation (including Bills and Statutory Instruments)

1. Adoption Acts, 1952-91
2. Adoptive Leave Act 1995
3. Age of Majority Act, 1985
4. Child Care Act, 1991
5. Child Abduction and Enforcement of Custody Orders Act, 1991
6. Children Act, 1989
7. Criminal Evidence Act, 1992
8. Criminal Law (Sexual Offences) Act, 1993
9. Criminal Law (Suicide) Act, 1993
10. Domestic Violence Bill, 1995
11. Family Law Act, 1995
12. Employment Equality Act, 1977
13. Family Law (Maintenance of Spouse and Children) Act, 1976
14. Guardianship of Infants Act, 1964
15. Health Act, 1970
16. Intoxicating Liquor Act, 1988
17. Judicial Separation and Family Law Reform Act, 1989
18. Marriages Act, 1972
19. Mental Treatment Act, 1945
20. Prohibition of Incitement to Hatred Act, 1989
21. Protection of Young Persons (Employment) Act, 1977
22. Refugee Bill, 1994
23. Safety, Health and Welfare at Work Act, 1989
24. Social Welfare Consolidation Act, 1993
25. Status of Children Act, 1987
26. Tobacco (Health promotion and Protection) Act, 1988

B. Statistical Information

1. Department of Education - Statistical Report
2. Department of Health - Health Statistics.
3. Department of Social Welfare - Statistical Information on Social Welfare Services

C. Other Miscellaneous Documents

1. Bunreacht na hÉireann
2. Department of Education - Guidelines on Notification of Suspected Cases of Child Abuse Between Health Boards and Gardaí
3. Department of Education - Guidelines Towards a Positive Policy for School Behaviour and Discipline
4. Department of Education - Procedures for Dealing with Allegations or Suspicions of Child Abuse
5. Department of Education - School Attendance/Truancy Report
6. Department of Education - The Education of Traveller Children in National Schools Guidelines
7. Department of Health - Child Abuse Guidelines
8. Department of Health - Draft Guide to Standards in Children's Residential Centres, January 1995
9. Department of Health - Health Promotion Strategy, 1995
10. Department of Health - Health Strategy, 1994
11. Draft New Prison Rules
12. Kilkenny Incest Investigation Report
13. National Anti-Poverty Strategy
14. Report of the Special Education Review Committee
15. Report by the Combat Poverty Agency - The Cost of a Child
16. Report of the National Economic and Social Forum - Ending Long Term Unemployment
17. Report of the Task Force on the Travelling Community, 1995
18. White paper on Education, 1994
19. White Paper on New Mental Health Legislation

CONVENTION ON THE RIGHTS OF THE CHILD

PREAMBLE

The States Parties to the present Convention,

Considering that, in accordance with the principles pro-claimed in the charter of the United Nations, recognition of the inherent dignity and of the equal and inalienable rights of all members of the human family is the foundation of freedom, justice and peace in the world,

Bearing in mind that the peoples of the United Nations have, in the Charter, reaffirmed their faith in fundamental human rights and in the dignity and worth of the human person, and have determined to promote social progress and better standards of life in larger freedom,

Recognizing that the United Nations has, in the Universal Declaration of Human Rights and in the International Covenants on Human Rights, proclaimed and agreed that everyone is entitled to all the rights and freedoms set forth therein, without distinction of any kind, such as race, colour, sex, language, religion, political or other opinion, national or social origin, property, birth or other status,

Recalling that, in the Universal Declaration of Human Rights, the United Nations has proclaimed that childhood is entitled to special care and assistance,

Convinced that the family, as the fundamental group of society and the natural environment for the growth and well-being of all its members and particularly children, should be afforded the necessary protection and assistance so that it can fully assume its responsibilities within the community,

Recognizing that the child, for the full and harmonious development of his or her personality, should grow up in a family environment, in an atmosphere of happiness, love and understanding,

Considering that the child should be fully prepared to live an individual life in society, and brought up in the spirit of the ideals proclaimed in the Charter of the United Nations, and in particular in the spirit of peace, dignity, tolerance, freedom, equality and solidarity,

Bearing in mind that the need to extend particular care to the child has been stated in the Geneva Declaration of the rights of the Child of 1924 and in the Declaration of the Rights of the Child adopted by the General Assembly on 20 November 1959 and recognized in the universal Declaration of Human Rights, in the International Covenant on Civil and Political rights (in particular in articles 23 and 24), in the International Covenant on Economic, Social and Cultural Rights (in particular in article 10) and in the statutes and relevant instruments of specialized agencies and international organizations concerned with the welfare of children,

Bearing in mind that, as indicated in the Declaration of the Rights of the Child, "the child, by reason of his physical and mental immaturity, needs special safeguards and care, including appropriate legal protection, before as well as after birth",

Recalling the provisions of the Declaration on Social and Legal Principles relating to the Protection and Welfare of Children, with Special Reference to Foster Placement and Adoption Nationally and Internationally; the United Nations Standard Minimum Rules for the Administration of Juvenile Justice (The Beijing Rules); and the Declaration on the Protection of Women and Children in Emergency and Armed Conflict,

Recognizing that, in all countries in the world, there are children living in exceptionally difficult conditions, and that such children need special consideration,

Taking due account of the importance of the traditions and cultural values of each people for the protection and harmonious development of the child,

Recognizing the importance of international co-operation for improving the living conditions of children in every country, in particular in the developing countries,

Have agreed as follows:

ARTICLE 1

For the purposes of the present Convention, a child means every human being below the age of eighteen years unless, under the law applicable to the child, majority is attained earlier.

ARTICLE 2

1.   States Parties shall respect and ensure the rights set forth in the present Convention to each child within their jurisdiction without discrimination of any kind, irrespective of the child's or his or her parent's or legal guardian's race, colour, sex, language, religion, political or other opinion, national, ethnic or social origin, property, disability, birth or other status.

2.   States parties shall take all appropriate measures to ensure that the child is protected against all forms of discrimination or punishment on the basis of the status, activities, expressed opinions, or beliefs of the child's parents, legal guardians, or family members.

ARTICLE 3

1.   In all actions concerning children, whether undertaken by public or private social welfare institutions, courts of law, administrative authorities or legislative bodies, the best interests of the child shall be a primary consideration.

2.   States Parties undertake to ensure the child such protection and care as is necessary for his or her well-being, taking into account the rights and duties of his or her parents, legal guardians, or other individuals legally responsible for him or her, and, to this end, shall take all appropriate legislative and administrative measures.

3.   States Parties shall ensure that the institutions, services and facilities responsible for the care or protection of children shall conform with the standards established by competent authorities, particularly in the areas of safety, health, in the number and suitability of their staff, as well as competent supervision.

ARTICLE 4

States Parties shall undertake all appropriate legislative, administrative, and other measures for the implementation of the rights recognized in the present Convention. With regard to economic, social and cultural rights, States Parties shall undertake such measures to the maximum extent of their available resources and, where needed, within the framework of international co-operation.

ARTICLE 5

States Parties shall respect the responsibilities, rights and duties of parents or, where applicable, the members of the extended family or community as provided for by local custom, legal guardians or other persons legally responsible for the child, to provide, in a manner consistent with the evolving capacities of the child, appropriate direction and guidance in the exercise by the child of the rights recognized in the present Convention.

ARTICLE 6

1.   States Parties recognize that every child has the inherent right to life.

2.   States Parties shall ensure to the maximum extent possible the survival and development of the child.

ARTICLE 7

1.   The child shall be registered immediately after birth and shall have the right from birth to a name, the right to acquire a nationality and, as far as possible, the right to know and be cared for by his or her parents.

2.   States Parties shall ensure the implementation of these rights in accordance with their national law and their obligations under the relevant international instruments in this field, in particular where the child would otherwise be stateless.

ARTICLE 8

1.   States Parties undertake to respect the right of the child to preserve his or her identity, including nationality, name and family relations as recognized by law without unlawful interference.

2.   Where a child is illegally deprived of some or all of the elements of his or her identity, States Parties shall provide appropriate assistance and protection, with a view to speedily re-establishing his or her identity.

ARTICLE 9

1.   States Parties shall ensure that a child shall not be separated from his or her parents against their will, except when competent authorities subject to judicial review determine, in accordance with applicable law and

procedures, that such separation is necessary for the best interests of the child. Such determination may be necessary in a particular case such as one involving abuse or neglect of the child by the parents, or one where the parents are living separately and a decision must be made as to the child's place of residence.

2.   In any proceedings pursuant to paragraph 1 of the present article, all interested parties shall be given an opportunity to participate in the proceedings and make their views known.

3.   States Parties shall respect the right of the child who is separated from one or both parents to maintain personal relations and direct contact with both parents on a regular basis, except if it is contrary to the child's best interests.

4.   Where such separation results from any action initiated by a State Party, such as the detention, imprisonment, exile, deportation or death (including death arising form any cause while the person is in the custody of the State) of one or both parents or f the child, that State Party shall, upon request, provide the parents, the child or, if appropriate, another member of the family with the essential information concerning the whereabouts of the absent member(s) of the family unless the provision of the information would be detrimental to the well-being of the child. States Parties shall further ensure that the submission of such a request shall of itself entail no adverse consequences for the person(s) concerned.

ARTICLE 10

1.   In accordance with the obligation of States Parties under article 9, paragraph 1, applications by a child or his or her parents to enter or leave a State Party for the purpose of family reunification shall be dealt with by States Parties in a positive, humane and expeditious manner. States Parties shall further ensure that the submission of such a request shall entail no adverse consequences for the applicants and for the members of their family.

2.   A child whose parents reside in different States shall have the right to maintain on a regular basis, save in exceptional circumstances, personal relations and direct contacts with both parents. Towards that end and in accordance with the obligation of States Parties under article 9, paragraph 1, States parties shall respect the right of the child and his or her parents to leave any country, including their own, and to enter their own country. The right to leave any county shall be subject only to such restrictions as are prescribed by law and which are necessary to protect the national security, public order (ordre public), public health or morals or the rights and freedoms of others and are consistent with the other rights recognized in the present Convention.

ARTICLE 11

1.   States Parties shall take measures to combat the illicit transfer and non-return of children abroad.

2.   To this end, States Parties shall promote the conclusion of bilateral or multilateral agreements or multilateral agreements or accession to existing agreements.

ARTICLE 12

1.   States Parties shall assure to the child who is capable of forming his or her own views the right to express those views freely in all matters affecting the child, the views of the child being given due weight in accordance with the age and maturity of the child.

2.   For this purpose, the child shall in particular b provided the opportunity to be heard in any judicial and administrative proceedings affecting the child, either directly, or through a representative or an appropriate body, in a manner consistent with the procedural rules of national law.

ARTICLE 13

1.   The child shall have the right to freedom of expression; this right shall include freedom to seek, receive and impart information and ideas of all kinds, regardless of frontiers, either orally, in writing or in print, in the form of art, or through any other media of the child's choice.

2.   The exercise of this right may be subject to certain restrictions, but these shall only be such as are provided by law and are necessary:

a)   For respect of the rights or reputations of others; or
b)   For the protection of national security or of public order (ordre public), or of public health or morals.

ARTICLE 14

1.   States Parties shall respect the right of the child to freedom of thought, conscience and religion.

2.   States Parties shall respect the rights and duties of the parents and, when applicable, legal guardians, to provide direction of the child in the exercise of his or her right in a manner consistent with the evolving capacities of the child.

3.   Freedom to manifest one's religion or beliefs may be subject to such limitations as are prescribed by law and are necessary to protect public safety, order, health or morals, or the fundamental rights and freedoms of others.

ARTICLE 15

1.   States Parties recognize the rights of the child to freedom of association and to freedom of peaceful assembly.

2.   No restrictions may be placed on the exercise of these rights other than those imposed in conformity with the law and which are necessary in a democratic society in the interests of national security or public safety, public order (ordre public), the protection of public health or morals or the protection of the rights and freedom of others.

ARTICLE 16

1.   No child shall be subjected to arbitrary or unlawful interference with his or her privacy, family, home or correspondence, nor to unlawful attacks on his or her honour and reputation.

2.   The child has the right to the protection of the law against such interference or attacks.

ARTICLE 17

States Parties recognize the important function performed by the mass media and shall ensure that the child has access to information and material from a diversity of national and international sources, especially those aimed at the promotion of his or her social, spiritual and moral wellbeing and physical and mental health. To this end, States Parties shall:

a)   Encourage the mass media to disseminate information and material of social and cultural benefit to the child and in accordance with the spirit of article 29;
b)   Encourage international co-operation in the production, exchange and dissemination of such information and material form a diversity of cultural, natural and international sources;
c)   Encourage the production and dissemination of children's books;
d)   Encourage the mass media to have particular regard to the linguistic needs of the child who belongs to a minority group or who is indigenous;
e)   Encourage the development of appropriate guidelines for the protection of the child from information and material injurious to his or her well-being, bearing in mind the provisions of articles 13 and 18.

ARTICLE 18

1.   States Parties shall use their best efforts to ensure recognition of the principle that both parents have common responsibilities for he upbringing and development of the child. Parents, or as the case may be, legal guardians, have the primary responsibility for the upbringing and development of the child. The best interests of the child will be their basic concern.

2.   For the purpose of guaranteeing and promoting the rights set forth in the present Convention, States Parties shall render appropriate assistance to parents and legal guardians int he performance of their child-rearing responsibilities and shall ensure the development of institutions, facilities and services for the care of children.

3.   States Parties shall take all appropriate measures to ensure that children of working parents have the right to benefit from child-care services and facilities for which they are eligible.

ARTICLE 19

1.   States Parties shall take all appropriate legislative, administrative, social and educational measures to protect the child from all forms of physical or mental violence, injury or abuse, while in the care of parent(s), legal guardian(s) or any other person who has the care of the child.

2.   Such protective measures should, as appropriate, include effective procedures for the establishment of social programmes to provide necessary support for the child and or those who have the care of the child, as well as for other forms of prevention and for identification, reporting, referral, investigation, treatment and follow-up of instances of child maltreatment described heretofore, and, as appropriate, for judicial involvement.

ARTICLE 20

1.   A child temporarily or permanently deprived of his or her family environment, or in whose own best interests cannot be allowed to remain in that environment, shall be entitled to special protection and assistance provided by the State.

2.   States Parties shall in accordance with their national laws ensure alternative care for such a child.

3.   Such care could include, inter alia, foster placement, Kafalah of Islamic law, adoption or if necessary placement in suitable institutions for the care of children. When considering solutions, die regard shall be paid to the desirability of continuity in a child's upbringing and to the child's ethnic, religious, cultural, and linguistic background.

ARTICLE 21

States parties that recognize and/or permit the system of adoption shall ensure that the best interests of the child shall be the paramount consideration and they shall:

a)   Ensure that the adoption of a child is authorized only by competent authorises who determine, in accordance with applicable law and procedures and on the basis of all pertinent and reliable information, that the adoption is permissible in view of the child's status concerning parents, relatives and legal guardians and that, if required, the persons concerned have given their informed consent to the adoption on the basis of such counselling as may be necessary;
b)   Recognize that inter-country adoption may be considered as an alternative means of child care, if the child cannot be placed in a foster or an adoptive family or cannot in any suitable manner be cared for in the child's country of origin;
c)   Ensure that the child concerned by inter-country adoption enjoys safeguard and standards equivalent to those existing in the case of national adoption;
d)   Take all appropriate measures to ensure that, in inter-country adoption, the placement does not result in improper financial gain for those involved in it;
e)   Promote, where appropriate, the objectives of the present article by concluding bilateral or multilateral arrangements or agreements, and endeavour, within this framework, to ensure that the placement of the child in another country is carried out by competent authorities or organs.

ARTICLE 22

1.   States Parties shall take appropriate measures to ensure that a child who is seeking refugee status or who is considered a refugee in accordance with applicable international or domestic law and procedures shall, whether unaccompanied or accompanied by his or her parents or by any other person, receive appropriate protection and humanitarian assistance in the enjoyment of applicable rights set forth in the present Convention and in other international human rights or humanitarian instruments to which the said States are Parties.

2.   For this purpose, States Parties shall provide, as they consider appropriate, co-operation in any efforts by the United Nations and other competent intergovernmental organizations or non-governmental organizations cooperating with the United Nations to protect and assist such a child and to trace the parents of other members of the family of any refugee child in order to obtain information necessary for reunification with his or her family. In cases where no parents or other members of he family can be found, the child shall be accorded the same protection as any other child permanently or temporarily deprived of his or her family environment for any reason, as set forth in the present Convention.

ARTICLE 23

1.   States Parties recognize that a mentally or physically disabled child should enjoy a full and decent life, in conditions which ensure dignity, promote self-reliance and facilitate the child's active participation in the community.

2.   States Parties recognize the right of the disabled child to special care and shall encourage and ensure the extension, subject to available resources, to the eligible child and those responsible for his or her care, of assistance for which application is made and which is appropriate to the child's condition and to the

circumstances of the parents or others caring for the child.

3.   Recognizing the special needs of a disabled child, assistance extended in accordance with paragraph 2 of the present article shall be provided free of charge, whenever possible, taking into account the financial resources of the parents or others caring for the child, and shall be designed to ensure that the disabled child has effective access to and receives education, training, health care services, rehabilitation services, preparation for employment and recreation opportunities in a manner conducive to the child's achieving the fullest possible social integration and individual development, including his or her cultural and spiritual development.

4.   States Parties shall promote, int he spirit of international co-operation, the exchange of appropriate information in the field of preventive health care and of medical, psychological and functional treatment of disabled children, including dissemination of and access to information concerning methods of rehabilitation, education and vocational services, with the aim of enabling States Parties to improve their capabilities and skills and to widen their experience in these areas. In this regard, particular account shall be taken of the needs of developing countries.

ARTICLE 24

1.   States Parties recognize the right of the child to the enjoyment of the highest attainable standard of health and to facilities for the treatment of illness and rehabilitation of health. States Parties shall strive to ensure that no child is deprived of his or her right of access to such health care services.

2.   States Parties shall pursue full implementation of this right and, in particular, shall take appropriate measures:

a)   To diminish infant and child mortality;
b)   To ensure the provision of necessary medical assistance and health care to all children with emphasis on the development of primary health care;
c)   To combat disease and malnutrition, including within the framework of primary health care, through, inter alia, the application of readily available technology and through the provision of adequate nutritious foods and clean drinking water, taking into consideration the dangers and risks of environmental pollution;
e)   To ensure that all segments of society, in particular parents and children, are informed, have access to education and are supported int he use of basic knowledge of child health and nutrition, the advantages of breast-feeding, hygiene and environmental sanitation and the prevention of accidents;
f)   To develop preventive health care, guidance for parents and family planning education and services.

3.   States Parties shall take all effective and appropriate measures with a view to abolishing traditional practices prejudicial to the health of children.

4.   States Parties undertake to promote and encourage international co-operation with a view to achieving progressively the full realization of the right recognized in the present article. In this regard, particular account shall be taken of the needs of developing countries.

ARTICLE 25

1.   States Parties recognize the right of a child who has been placed by a competent authorises for the purposes of care, protection or treatment of his or her physical or mental health, to a periodic review of the treatment provided to the child and all other circumstances relevant to his or her placement.

ARTICLE 26

1.   States Parties shall recognize for every child the right to benefit from social security, including social insurance, and shall take the necessary measures to achieve the full realization of this right in accordance with their national law.

2.   The benefits should, where appropriate, be granted, taking into account the resources and the circumstances of the child and persons having responsibility for the maintenance of the child, as well as any other consideration relevant to an application for benefits made by or on behalf of the child.

ARTICLE 27

1.   States Parties recognize the right of every child to a standard of living adequate for the child's physical, mental, spiritual, moral and social development.

2.   The parent(s) or others responsible for the child have the primary responsibility to secure, within their

abilities and financial capacities, the conditions of living necessary for the child's development.

3.   States Parties, in accordance with national conditions and within their means, shall take appropriate measures to assist parents and others responsible for the child to implement this right and shall in case of need provide material assistance and support programmes, particularly with regard to nutrition, clothing and housing.

4.   States Parties shall take all appropriate measures to secure the recovery of maintenance for the child from the parents or other persons having financial responsibility for the child, both within the State Party and from abroad. In particular, where the person having financial responsibility for the child lives in a State different from that of the child, States Parties shall promote the accession to international agreements or the conclusion of such agreements, as well as the making of other appropriate arrangements.

ARTICLE 28

1.   States Parties recognize the right of the child to education, and with a view to achieving this right progressively and on the basis of equal opportunity, they shall, in particular:

a)   make primary education compulsory and available free to all;
b)   Encourage the development of different forms of secondary education, including general and vocational education, make them available and accessible to every child, and take appropriate measures such as the introduction of free education and offering financial assistance in case of need;
c)   Make higher education accessible to all of the basis of capacity by every appropriate means;
d)   Make educational and vocational information and guidance available and accessible to all children;
e)   Take measures to encourage regular attendance at schools and the reduction of drop-out rates.

2.   States Parties shall take all appropriate measures to ensure that school discipline is administered in a manner consistent with the child's human dignity and in conformity with the present Convention.

3.   States Parties shall promote and encourage international co-operation in matters relating to education, in particular with a view to contributing to the elimination of ignorance and illiteracy throughout the world and facilitating access to scientific and technical knowledge and modern teaching methods. In this regard, particular account shall be taken of the needs of developing countries.

ARTICLE 29

1.   States parties agree that the education of the child shall be directed to:

a)   The development of the child's personality, talents and mental and physical abilities to their fullest potential;
b)   The development of respect for human rights and fundamental freedoms, and for the principles enshrined in the Charter of the United Nations;
c)   The development of respect for the child's parents, his or her own cultural identity, language and values, for the national values of the country in which the child is living, the county from which he or she may originate, and for civilizations different from his or her own;
d)   The preparation of the child for responsible life in a free society, in the spirit of understanding, peace, tolerance, equality of sexes, and friendship among all peoples, ethnic, national and religious groups and persons of indigenous origin;
e)   The development of respect for the natural environment.

2.   No part of the present article or article 28 shall be construed so as to interfere with the liberty of individuals and bodies to establish and direct educational institutions, subject always to the observance of the principles set forth in paragraph 1 of the present article and to the requirements that the education given in such institutions shall conform to such minimum standards as may be laid down by the State.

ARTICLE 30

In those States in which ethnic, religious or linguistic minorities or persons of indigenous origin exist, a child belonging to such a minority or who is indigenous shall not be denied the right, in community with other members of his or her group, to enjoy his or her own culture, to profess and practise his or her own religion, or to use his or her own language.

ARTICLE 31

1.   States Parties recognize the right of the child to rest and leisure, to engage in play and recreational activities appropriate tot he age of the child and to participate freely in cultural life and the arts.

2.   States Parties hall respect and promote the right of the child to participate fully in cultural and artistic life and shall encourage the provision of appropriate and equal opportunities for cultural, artistic, recreational and leisure activity.

ARTICLE 32

1.   States parties recognize the right of the child to be protected from economic exploitation and from performing any work that is likely to be hazardous or to interfere with the child's education, or to be harmful to the child's health or physical, mental, spiritual, moral or social development.

2.   States Parties shall take legislative, administrative, social and educational measures to ensure the implementation of the present article. To this end, and having regard tot he relevant provisions of other international instruments, States Parties shall in particular:

a)   Provide for a minimum age or minimum ages for admission to employment;
b)   Provide for appropriate regulation of the hours and conditions of employment;
c)   Provide for appropriate penalties or other sanctions to ensure the effective enforcement of the present article.

ARTICLE 33

States Parties shall take all appropriate measures, including legislative, administrative, social and educational measures, to protect children form the illicit use of narcotic drugs and psychotropic substances as defined in the relevant international treaties, and to prevent the use of children in the illicit production and trafficking of such substances.

ARTICLE 34

States Parties undertake to protect the child from all forms of sexual exploitation and sexual abuse. For these purposes, States Parties shall in particular take all appropriate national, bilateral and multilateral measures to prevent:

a)   The inducement or coercion of a child to engage in any unlawful sexual activity;
b)   The exploitative use of children in prostitution or other unlawful sexual practices;
c)   The exploitative use of children in pornographic performances and materials.

ARTICLE 35

States Parties shall take all appropriate national, bilateral and multilateral measures to prevent the abduction of, the sale of or traffic in children for any purpose or in any form.

ARTICLE 36

States Parties shall protect the child against all other forms of exploitation prejudicial to any aspects of the child's welfare.

ARTICLE 37

States Parties shall ensure that:

a)   No child shall be subjected to torture or other cruel, in human or degrading treatment or punishment. Neither capital punishment nor life imprisonment without possibility of release shall be imposed for offences committed by persons below eighteen years of age;
b)   No child shall be deprived of his or her liberty unlawfully or arbitrarily. The arrest, detention or imprisonment of a child shall be in conformity with the law and shall be used only as a measure or last resort and for the shortest appropriate period of time;
c)   Every child deprived of liberty shall be treated with humanity and respect for the inherent dignity of the human person, and in a manner which takes into account the needs of persons of his or her age, in particular, every child deprived of liberty shall be separated from adults unless it is considered in the child's best interest not to do so and shall have the right to maintain with his or her family through correspondence and visits, save in exceptional circumstances;
d)   Every child deprived of his or her liberty shall have the right to prompt access to legal and other appropriate assistance, as well as the right to challenge the legality of the deprivation of his or her liberty before a court or other competent, independent and impartial authority, and to a prompt decision on any such action.

ARTICLE 38

1.   States Parties undertake to respect and to ensure respect for rules of international humanitarian law applicable to them in armed conflicts which are relevant to the child.

2.   States Parties shall take all feasible measures to ensure that persons who have not attained the age of fifteen years do not take a direct part in hostilities.

3.   States Parties shall refrain from recruiting any person who has not attained the age of fifteen years into their armed forces. In recruiting among those person s who have attained the age of fifteen years but who have not attained the age of eighteen years, States Parties shall endeavour to give priority to those who are oldest.

4.   In accordance with their obligations under international humanitarian law to protect the civilian population in armed conflicts, States Parties shall take all feasible measures to ensure protection and care of children who are affected by an armed conflict.

ARTICLE 39

States Parties shall take all appropriate measures to promote physical and psychological recovery and social reintegration of a child victim of: any form of neglect, exploitation, or abuse; torture or any other form of cruel, in human or degrading treatment or punishment; or armed conflicts. Such recovery and reintegration shall take place in an environment which fosters the health, self-respect and dignity of the child.

ARTICLE 40

1.   States Parties recognize the right of every child alleged as, accused of, or recognized as having infringed the penal law to be treated in a manner consistent with the promotion of the child's sense of dignity and worth, which reinforces the child's respect for the human rights and fundamental freedoms of others and which takes into account the child's age and the desirability of promoting the child's reintegration and the child's assuming a constructive role in society.

2.   To this end, and having regard to the relevant provisions of international instruments, States Parties shall, in particular, ensure that:

a)   No child shall be alleged as, be accused of, or recognized as having infringed the penal law by reason of acts or omissions that were not prohibited by national or international law at the time they were committed;
b)   Every child alleged as or accused of having infringed the penal law has at least the following guarantees:
   i)   To be presumed innocent until proven guilty according to law;
   ii)   To be informed promptly and directly of the charges against him or her, and, if appropriate, through his or her parents or legal guardians, and to have legal or other appropriate assistance in the preparation and presentation of his or her defence;
   iii)   To have the matter determined without delay by a competent, independent and impartial authority or judicial body in a fair hearing according to law, in the presence of legal or other appropriate assistance and, unless it is considered not to be in the best interest of the child, in particular, taking into account his or her age or situation, his or her parents or legal guardians;
   iv)   Not to be compelled to give testimony or to confess guilt; to examine or have examined adverse witnesses and to obtain the participation and examination of witness on his or her behalf under conditions of equality;
   v)   If considered to have infringed the penal law, to have this decision and any measures imposed in consequence thereof reviewed by a higher competent, independent and impartial authority or judicial body according to law;
   vi)   To have the free assistance of an interpreter if the child cannot understand or speak the language used;
   vii)   To have his or her privacy fully respected at all stages of the proceedings.

3.   States Parties shall seek to promote the establishment of laws, procedures, authorities and institutions specifically applicable to children alleged as, accused of, or recognized as having
infringed the penal law, and, in particular;

a)   The establishment of a minimum age below which children shall be presumed not to have the capacity to infringe the penal law;
b)   Whenever appropriate and desirable, measures for dealing with such children without resorting to judicial proceedings, providing that human rights and legal safeguards are fully respected.

4.   A variety of dispositions, such as care, guidance and supervision orders; counselling; probation; foster

care; education and vocational training programmes and other alternatives to institutional care shall be available to ensure that children are dealt with in a manner appropriate to their well-being and proportionate both to their circumstances and the offence.

ARTICLE 41

Nothing in the present Convention shall affect any provisions which are more conducive tot he realization of the rights of the child and which may be contained in:

a)   The law of a State Party; or
b)   International law in force for that State.

ARTICLE 42

States Parties undertake to make the principles and provisions of the Convention widely known, by appropriate and active means, to adults and children alike.

ARTICLE 43

1.   For the purpose of examining the progress made by States Parties in achieving the realization of the obligations undertaken in the present Convention, there shall be established a Committee on the Rights of the Child, which shall carry out the functions hereinafter provided.

2.   The Committee shall consist of ten experts of high moral standing and recognized competence in the field covered by this Convention. The members of the Committee shall be elected by States Parties from among their nationals and shall serve in their personal capacity, consideration being given to equitable geographical distribution, as well as to the principal legal systems.

3.   The members of the Committee shall be elected by secret ballot from a list of persons nominated by States Parties. Each State Party may nominate one person from among its own nationals.

4.   The initial election of the Committee shall be held no later than six months after the date of the entry into force of the present Convention and thereafter every second year. At least four months before the date of each election, the Secretary-General of the United Nations shall address a letter to States Parties inviting them to submit their nominations within two months. The Secretary-General shall subsequently prepare a list in alphabetical order of all persons thus nominated, indicating States Parties which have nominated them, and shall submit it to the States Parties to the present Convention.

5.   The elections shall be held at meetings of States Parties convened by the Secretary-General at united Nations Headquarters. At those meetings, for which two thirds of States Parties shall constitute a quorum, the persons elected to the Committee shall be those who obtain the largest number of votes and an absolute majority of the votes of the representatives of States Parties present and voting.

6.   The members of the Committee shall be elected for a term of four years. They shall be eligible for re-election if renominated. The term of five of the members elected at the first election shall expire at the end of two years; immediately after the first election, the names of these five members shall be chosen by lot by the Chairman of the meeting.

7.   If a member of the Committee dies or resigns or declares that for any other cause he or she can no longer perform the duties of the Committee, the State Party which nominated the member shall appoint another expert from among its nationals to serve for the remainder of the term, subject to the approval of the Committee.

8.   The Committee shall establish its own rules of procedure.

9.   The Committee shall elect its officers for a period of two years.

10.   The meeting of the Committee shall normally be held at United Nations Headquarters or at any other convenient place as determined by the Committee. The Committee shall normally meet annually. The duration of the meetings of the Committee shall be determined, and reviewed, if necessary, by a meeting of the States Parties of the present Convention, subject to the approval of the General Assembly.

11.   The Secretary-General of the United Nations shall provide the necessary staff nd facilities for the effective performance of the functions of the Committee under the present Convention.

12.   With the approval of the General Assembly, the members of the Committee established under the

present Convention shall receive emoluments from United Nations resources on such terms and conditions as the Assembly may decide.

ARTICLE 44

1.   States Parties undertake to submit to the Committee, through the Secretary-General of the United Nations, reports on the measures they have adopted which give effect to the rights recognized herein and on the progress made on the enjoyment of those rights:

a)   Within two years of the entry into force of the Convention for the Stare party concerned;
b)   Thereafter every five years.

2.   Reports made under the present article shall indicate factors and difficulties, if any, affecting the degree of fulfilment of the obligations under the present Convention. Reports shall also contain sufficient information to provide the Committee with a comprehensive understanding of the implementation of the Convention in the country concerned.

3.   A State Party which has submitted a comprehensive initial report to the Committee need not, in its subsequent reports submitted in accordance with paragraph 1 (b) of the present article, repeat basic information previously provided.

4.   The Committee may request from States Parties further information relevant to the implementation of the Convention.

5.   The Committee shall submit to the General Assembly, through the Economic and Social Council, every two years, reports on its activities.

6.   States Parties shall make their reports widely available to the public in their own countries.

ARTICLE 45

In order to foster the effective implementation of the Convention and to encourage international co-operation in the field covered by the Convention:

a)   The specialized agencies, the United Nations Children's Fund, and other United Nations organs shall be entitled to be represented at the consideration of the implementation of such provisions of the present Convention as fall within the scope of their mandate. The Committee may invite the specialized agencies, the United Nations Children's Fund and other competent bodies as it may consider appropriate to provide expert advice on the implementation of the Convention in areas falling within the scope of their respective mandates. The Committee may invite the specialized agencies, the United Nations Children's Fund, and other United Nations organs to submit reports on the implementation of the Convention in areas falling within the scope of their activities;
b)   The Committee shall transmit, as it may consider appropriate, to the specialized agencies, the United nations Children's Fund and other competent bodies, any reports from States parties that contain a request, or indicate a need, for technical advice or assistance, along with the Committee's observations and suggestions, if any, on these requests or indications;
c)   The Committee may recommend to the General Assembly to request the Secretary-General to undertake on its behalf studies on specific issues relating to the rights of the child;
d)   The Committee may make suggestions and general recommendations based on information received pursuant to articles 44 and 45 of the present Convention. Such suggestion and general recommendations shall be transmitted to any State Party concerned and reported to the General Assembly, together with comments, if any, from States Parties.

ARTICLE 46

The present Convention shall be open for signature by all States.

ARTICLE 47

The present Convention is subject to ratification. Instruments of ratification shall be deposited with the Secretary-General of the United Nations.

ARTICLE 48

The present Convention shall remain open for accession by any State.. The instruments of accession shall be deposited with the Secretary-General of the United Nations.

ARTICLE 49

1.   The present Convention shall enter into force on the thirtieth day following the date of deposit with the Secretary-General of the United Nations of the twentieth instrument of ratification or accession.

2.   For each State ratifying or acceding to the Convention after the deposit of the twentieth instrument of ratification or accession, the Convention shall enter into force on the thirtieth day after the deposit by such State of its instrument of ratification or accession.

ARTICLE 50

1.   Any State Party may propose an amendment and file it with the Secretary-General of the United Nations. The Secretary-General shall thereupon communicate the proposed amendment to States Parties, with a request that they indicate whether they favour a conference of States Parties for the purpose of considering and voting upon the proposals. In the event that, within four months from the date of such communication, at least one third of the States Parties favour such a conference, the Secretary-General shall convene the conference under the auspices of the United Nations. Any amendment adopted by a majority of States Parties present and voting at the conference shall be submitted to the General Assembly for approval.

2.   An amendment adopted in accordance with paragraph 1 of the present article shall enter into force when it has been approved by the General Assembly of the United Nations and accepted by a two-thirds majority of States Parties.

3.   When an amendment enters into force, it shall be binding on those States Parties which have accepted it, other States Parties still being bound by the provisions of the present Convention and any earlier amendments which they have accepted.

ARTICLE 51

1.   The Secretary-General of the United Nations shall receive and circulate to all States the text of reservations made by States at the time of ratification or accession.

2.   A reservation incompatible with the object and purpose of the present Convention shall not be permitted.

3.   Reservations may be withdrawn at any time by notification to that effect addressed to the Secretary-General of the United Nations, who shall then inform all States. Such notification shall take effect on the date on which it is received by the Secretary-General.

ARTICLE 52

A State Party may denounce the present Convention by written notification tot he Secretary-General of the United Nations, who shall then inform all States. Such notification shall take effect on the date on which it is received by the Secretary-General.

ARTICLE 53

the Secretary-General of the United Nations is designated as the depositary of the present Convention.

ARTICLE 54

The original of the present Convention, of which the Arabic, Chinese, English, French, Russian and Spanish texts are equally authentic, shall be deposited with the Secretary-General of the United Nations.

IN WITNESS THEREOF the undersigned plenipotentiaries, being duly authorized thereto by their respective Governments, have signed the present Convention.